RICHER THAN YOU DREAMED

RICHER THAN YOU DREAMED

HOW TO
TAKE CONTROL OF YOUR
TWO-INCOME FAMILY'S FINANCES

Kathryn Maxwell, Steven Sisgold, and Thomas E. Chesus

CLARKSON POTTER/PUBLISHERS
NEW YORK

Published by Clarkson N. Potter, Inc.,
201 East 50th Street,
New York, New York 10022.
Member of the Crown Publishing Group.

CLARKSON N. POTTER, POTTER, and colophon are trademarks of
Clarkson N. Potter, Inc.

Manufactured in the United States of America

Designed by Katy Riegel

Library of Congress Cataloging-in-Publication Data
Maxwell, Kathryn.
   Richer than you dreamed : how to take control of your two-income
family's finances / Kathryn Maxwell, Steven Sisgold, and Thomas E. Chesus.
      p.   cm.
   1. Dual-career families—Finance, Personal.   I. Sisgold, Steven.
II. Chesus, Thomas E.   III. Title.
HG179.M36   1992
332.024—dc20   91-23142
                                                             CIP

ISBN 0-517-57432-2

10 9 8 7 6 5 4 3 2 1

First Edition

To our loving parents, Alfred and Doris McCormick, Morris and Tillye Sisgold, and Roman and Mary Chesus, for teaching us sound values and encouraging us to pursue our dreams; and to Jesse Sisgold for his love and inspiration

What is life, without a dream?
                    —Edmond Rostand

As you establish new structures, outcomes
which in the past may have seemed elusive
and impossible to create can now be created
easily, organically, and quite often
effortlessly.
                    —Robert Fritz,
                      The Path of Least Resistance

CONTENTS

ACKNOWLEDGMENTS

We are deeply grateful to our clients for their courage and willingness to take the necessary steps toward a more harmonious relationship with each other and their finances.

We sincerely appreciate and applaud the creativity and writing skills of Katie Brown. Her energy and enthusiasm were invaluable in the writing of this book.

We also thank our editors at Clarkson Potter, Lauren Shakely and Alexandra Enders, for believing in us, providing valuable editorial contributions, and encouraging us to express our ideas.

PREFACE

In our ten years of helping families manage their money, we encountered again and again the same problems that kept people from achieving financial security. These common experiences, lack of knowledge and frustration, inspired us to offer to a wider audience the tools that helped our clients.

This book is arranged from the general to the particular. First, we describe the forces that have shaped our generation's perceptions about money. Then, we talk about goals and aspirations and your feelings about money. Finally, we discuss specifics of healthy cash flow management and achieving your goals.

At the end of each chapter is a checkpoint that summarizes the chapter's main points and provides exercises to help you discuss those issues as they affect your life. Often the exercise sections refer to charts in the appendix. These charts are similar to the ones we provide our clients as they create a cash flow plan. You may want to photocopy these charts and keep them in appropriately labeled folders. The forms are also easily adaptable to any common computer spreadsheet program.

However you decide to approach the book—from simply reading to completing all of the exercises—we hope you will keep in mind that the key to solving any problem or ending any struggle is communication. It is our hope that by reading this book you will not only take charge of your financial life, but you will refresh and revitalize your relationship.

RICHER THAN YOU DREAMED

INTRODUCTION

The Subtle Revolution

here is almost nothing so exciting as falling in
love, indulging in fantasies of the perfect life together, making the commitment, getting married,
and beginning to build your dreams. The togeth-
erness is exhilarating. And while you may not be
the least bit interested in talking about finances, when you set
up house together you notice one dramatic change: your income
has increased, perhaps even doubled as a two-career couple.
It's like a bonus for getting married.

The tidal wave of two-income families has produced what the
Urban Institute, a Washington, D.C., research center, has
termed a "subtle revolution." The gradual but profound shift in
life patterns has permanently changed the way most American
couples think about marriage, children, sex, work, goals, family, self, and money.

By coming together as a two-income family, you're suddenly
richer than you dreamed. You have it made. Not only are you
happy, but you have the means to enjoy the good life. Compare
yourself to this statistic: the Bureau of Labor Statistics reported
that in 1988 a fifth of the nation's households earned at least

$55,900. Together, the two of you have secured a place among the wealthiest 20 percent of the nation. And with that comfortable combined income, you dive into building a life together, with new furniture, romantic vacations, dinners out (because with two jobs you're both too busy and tired at the end of the day to bother with cooking), cozy weekend bed-and-breakfast getaways, symphony tickets, and doing just about anything you want because now you are a two-paycheck family. You take the occasion and the liberty to pursue a lifetime filled with fun and expense.

But gradually a shadow creeps up on you: debt. You're spending more each month than you bring in, and you wonder what has happened to that bank deposit that should be fat because you have two incomes. You rationalize: "Well, we're busy building our life, and we can handle it. We're both on steep earning curves. We'll catch up." Meanwhile, the banks keep sending credit cards and increasing your limits on the other cards—you *must* be able to afford it or the banks wouldn't take the chance on you.

Eventually, you may start a family—another dream you've always had. Your kids are the center of your life, and you want to give them everything that you had and more. It's such a delight to watch them develop, and you are thrilled to be able to give them so much. But money's getting tighter and that lingering debt begins to get out of hand. Why should this be happening to you? You're intelligent and successful, a career-and-family-oriented couple. You've been working hard to have what you want and to give your children what they want and need. But every month you're faced with the gnawing realization that your financial situation is getting more difficult to manage. You have encountered the illusion of affluence and are beginning to suffer the consequences. Finally, you have to admit you're poorer than you think.

What has happened is simply this: you have run up against the extra consumer costs of having a two-paycheck family. When both spouses work, unanticipated extra costs arise. These costs may be absolutely necessary or simply desired, but either way, they are increased costs. And that's what really adds up in the end. The extra costs arise in four main areas:

- The extra costs of the second job
- The extra costs of raising kids
- The extra costs of the illusion of affluence
- The extra costs of financial "rights"

Don't panic. It's not the end of the world, and you're not the only couple in this mess. It sounds trite, but it's true. Most families encounter cash flow problems and rising costs, and our society and economy significantly influence these conditions. Just look at the federal deficit. But better than misery loving company is the fact that you *can* overcome these troubles, get your finances in order, live within your means, and finally, have what it is you really want out of life. Most people would prefer to have healthy cash flow, complete with multipurpose savings accounts and funds for investments. There is a sane and comfortable way to achieve this financial nirvana.

Developing a Plan

In this book, we show you how to take control of your financial life and again become richer than you dreamed. We're not talking about pie-in-the-sky number crunching and phantom income that improves your family's balance sheet. We're talking about paying your bills on time, saving enough money for periodic expenses, and effectively reducing your debt. We'll show you how to liberate money that now goes into servicing your debt and put it to work. In the last ten years, thousands of couples have come through our offices—each of them motivated and able to make positive changes toward their financial peace of mind.

We have developed a plan designed to show you how much you really spend, where you spend it, and how to balance your spending in harmony with what you earn. By developing your own plan as you read this book and sticking to it, you will

- Know where your money goes
- Learn techniques for making your cash flow work
- Create a savings plan that works
- Turn the debt tide with a well-run debt elimination plan and pay it all off
- Assess how much your lifestyle costs and how to modify it
- Evaluate what income targets and goals will truly succeed for you

As anyone with responsibilities knows, placing blame on anyone or any institution is pointless. We believe that with determination and a little hard work you can put Pandora's demons back into the box. Overall, most two-income couples are already managing their family finances fairly well—bills generally get paid; the savings account may be small, but at least it's a start; and a few shares of stock are the foundation for a portfolio. It's really the specter of the future—the looming debt, anxiety about sending the kids to college, or planning for a retirement that is unsettling.

What we have found is that most people have trouble with money because they fail to recognize that it is always an emotional issue as well as a practical matter. More couples fight over money than any other topic—sex and love included. Instead of forging a partnership, identifying goals, and tailoring a plan to achieve mutual dreams, many couples blame each other and wrangle about expenditures at random—or, worse for their budget and their marriage, avoid talking about it at all. This might have worked for our parents, who were mostly one-income families with simple in-and-out cash flow, but it doesn't work in today's two-income family. What we swept under the rug yesterday comes creeping out to haunt us today.

We don't expect you to chop up your credit cards, start shopping at closeout sales, eat macaroni and cheese with ketchup, drink generic beer, take a vacation in a podunk town, turn down the heat to 50 degrees in the winter, or live by candlelight. Those extremist measures turn people into misers—not happy families. Above all, our purpose in writing this book is to make your life easier, happier, and more fulfilling by helping you communicate with each other, set your common goals, and direct your energy into achieving those goals with your cash flow under control.

We want you to have fun, not cringe every time the subject of money comes up. It'll take some work on your part, but if you schedule a small amount of time each month to manage and review your situation and your family financial plan, you'll be amazed at how simple and painless the process can be.

For each of our clients, we set up a custom-designed plan organized to help manage cash flow effectively, pay bills on time, and save money. A bonus is that the plan is a holding bin for other financial information, such as financial statements and insurance coverage.

Habit and behavior dramatically affect families' spending and saving practices. You will need to modify those behaviors and gear yourself toward a new and preferred set of habits that will intrinsically contribute to the desired result—healthy cash flow and a happy family. Communicate constructively with your spouse about family money matters and you'll be able to improve and strengthen the health of your family cash flow. With genuine desires and shared determination, you can become richer than you dreamed.

1

The First
Credit Generation

Baby boomers are lucky. With the exception of an economic slump here and there, we grew up in a prosperous time. Many of us lived in single-family homes owned by our parents, we received new bicycles on our birthdays, pursued hobbies, and collected an allowance or worked around the house or neighborhood to earn a little extra money. We expected to go to college with support from our parents and to graduate into our chosen careers.

We had a nearly carefree existence, a contrast to our parents' upbringing. Many of them worked as children during the Great Depression or learned to ration during World War II. We have all heard dramatic stories about how they trudged barefoot to school in hip-deep snow—five miles each way—and then ran home to milk the cow, put up preserves, darn socks, and, of course, study until midnight—by lantern light.

Most of our parents obviously never did all or any of that, but it was one way of letting us know that we had it better than they did. And we did. We had the advantage of growing up in the economic warm sun of the immediate postwar era.

We pursued our ideals, which included the pursuit of comfortable living.

Statistics abound to show us how lucky we really are. In the 1930 Census, 43.2 percent of all married couples said they owned their own homes. By 1960, the figure had risen to 67.1 percent. In other words, roughly two-thirds of baby boomers grew up in homes owned by their parents. We had a more comfortable public education, too. Most of us also remember our parents telling us they had to buy their own school supplies. Remember how we got a new box of crayons, a new eraser, and a new no. 2 pencil each September? School budgets per child were more generous when we were in school. The government increased its spending per student at an average rate of 30 percent per decade beginning in 1940, compared with an increase of 8.4 percent from 1929 to 1940. Spending for elementary and secondary education rose from 2.3 percent of the gross national product (GNP) in 1940, six years before the baby boom generation technically began, to 4.1 percent of the GNP in 1970, when many of us were still attending those schools.

More post–World War II Americans have benefited from higher education, too. Twice as many Americans aged twenty-five to thirty-four had college educations in 1980 (14.8 percent) as they did in 1950 (7.4 percent). The percentage of Americans aged twenty-five to thirty-four with high school degrees rocketed from 49 percent in 1950 to 85.5 percent in 1980. In actual terms, the number seems even more staggering: in 1930, the nation's universities conferred 122,000 bachelor's degrees. By 1940, when the parents of the first baby boomers were of college age, the number of bachelor's degrees rose to 187,000. By 1950, the number had jumped to 432,000, a peak not surpassed again until 1964. By 1968, when the first baby boomers were graduating from college, the number of degrees conferred rose to 827,000. These numbers provide clear evidence of our parents' and the government's commitment to our higher education. Our generation really is the first job-seeking group that is *expected* to have a college degree, and many employers *prefer* us to have postgraduate degrees.

We certainly can't complain about our generation's achievements. But for many of us, growing up was more of a party than a struggle: we became used to having what we wanted, within reason, or at least what we needed. As a result, we became lifestyle oriented. Although fostered by our parents' post–World War II success and comfort, the lifestyle approach is the polar opposite of our parents' view of the world. They weren't about to put themselves in a position to suffer the slings and arrows of another economic debacle: every decision they made reflected the primary goal of security. Buying a house meant security. Getting a retirement fund or nest egg in the bank meant security. Sticking with the same job or career, even if you hated it, meant security. Rather than enjoy the kind of carefree existence we do, our parents laid up reserves for an uncertain future, preparing for a calamity that, for most of them, never came. Our parents saved first, then purchased with cash.

We grew up with the stability that was spawned from our parents' drive to be secure. That security likely engendered the false belief that all families had the same happy level of affluence, along with the conviction that financial security is a given American right. What we have ultimately had to face as adults is the realization that economic reality has shifted, and our expectations will have to shift too, if we are to achieve security of our own. As it is, many of us wake up one day when we're in our forties and say, "Maybe I should start thinking about my retirement. Maybe I should open an IRA." Accustomed to comfortable living, we buy before we think, emptying our bank accounts like kids in a candy store. We charge ahead as high-speed credit consumers. We want it, we buy it. After all, most of us got our first credit cards in college, often without asking the parents who supported us or the bank that mailed the cards. Now many couples with children are still enjoying plush lifestyles, continuing to spend as they did before they had children, only more so.

The American personal savings rate points out the problem very well. From 1980 to 1989, we averaged a personal savings rate of 5.4 percent of disposable income. That compares with 7.9 percent from 1970 to 1979. Parents of the first baby boomers saved as much as 25 percent of their income during World War II. From 1950 to 1970, the average savings rate was 6.8 percent. This dramatic shift in the savings rate clearly illustrates the change from our parents' prudent behavior as savers and investors to our have-it-now habits as spenders and consumers.

Empirically, however, we've done worse. During the raging bull market that came to a dead halt in 1987, savings rates plummeted while many investors looked to stocks for the best return on their dollars. In 1987, the year of bull-market frenzy, we saved only 3.2 percent of our disposable income. In the last full quarter before the crash, we saved only 1.8 percent. While the other stock market's performance stacked record upon record, the frenzy that fed the fire was greed: the stock market had become a get-rich-quick scheme rather than a long-term investment. Instead of saving for the long haul, many small investors started taking short trips on Wall Street.

The savings habits of Americans are even less impressive when compared with those of other nations. The Organization for Economic Cooperation and Development in Washington, D.C., reports that net household savings as a percent of disposable household income (as opposed to the savings rate for individuals) for Americans in 1988 was 4.4 percent. That compares with 15.2 percent for the Japanese, 12.6 percent for Germans, and 16.1 percent for the Irish. Our lack of savings is also one of the primary forces behind our mounting personal debt. While we could and should save for such anticipated annual expenses as clothes, gifts, travel, furniture, professional services, and taxes, we often turn to credit cards or personal loans to carry the burden. Each year, the debt load becomes heavier, further threatening our tenuous security.

Credit as a Way of Life

Compounding the effect of our dismal savings rate is the surge in the use of credit cards. Managing our finances would be much less difficult had we not accepted so many tempting offers for credit that came in the mail. Credit cards made our lifestyles possible, and finance companies have marketed themselves aggressively.

Our parents didn't have credit cards. They bought with cash. At most, they deferred payment until the end of the month by using a department store account, or they used layaway plans. With few exceptions, if you didn't have the cash, you didn't buy furniture, clothes, or gourmet cookware. Nobody slapped down that little piece of plastic on a store counter. Clerks had no reason to ask, "Cash or charge?" Now, credit cards are offered as early as college, and even children sometimes have use of a parent's card. We started using cards almost as soon as we were consumers, and we've kept using them. And our credit limits keep rising because we're such good customers. If credit cards didn't exist, or weren't so easy to procure, we wouldn't have cultivated the lifestyles we now enjoy.

The first credit card was issued in 1914 by Western Union to its preferred customers, allowing them to defer payment with no interest charged. During the first half of the century, other businesses, such as hotels, department stores, and gasoline companies, issued charge cards to their customers. In 1950, Diners Club offered the first card accepted by a variety of merchants, not just the gas company or the department store. Cardholders were billed monthly and were required to pay the full balance each month. In 1951, Franklin National Bank on Long Island issued a charge card that was accepted by local merchants, and soon about a hundred other regional banks followed suit. Still, no fees or interest were charged to cardholders. The cards remained a deferred payment system.

The historic moment came in the late 1950s. Bank of America, a California bank with the largest potential market for charge cards, issued its first card in 1958 with a new twist. The BankAmericard offered *credit* cards.

There you have it. Our parents were already adults with children when credit cards first became available and adults with grown children by the time they became widespread. That makes us the first generation to grow up in a society that very quickly has become credit based. By 1970, more than fourteen hundred banks offered either BankAmericard (which became Visa in 1977) or Master Charge (which later became Master-Card), with a total outstanding balance of $3.8 billion. By 1988, Visa U.S.A. alone had five thousand member financial institutions, all issuing cards, often to the same subscribers. The volume of charges on the Discover card, introduced in 1986, increased sixfold by 1988. In the United States, bank credit card transactions total about $250 billion a year, about 10.5 percent of total U.S. consumer payments of $3.5 trillion.

Well, 10 percent sounds modest, you might be thinking. Still, it's 10 percent when only twenty years ago credit card purchases were a minuscule portion of total purchases. And Visa, for one, is aggressively seeking ways to tap the huge potential market of people who have resisted cards so far, of people who used them in limited ways, and for uses that have never been applied before: checking out of the hospital, buying weekly groceries, or paying for children's college educations.

Credit cards already have contributed significantly to the total debt level. In 1950, just before charge cards became credit cards, consumer debt was $13.9 billion. In 1980, total consumer debt had catapulted to $298.9 billion. By 1989, the number had more than *doubled* to $699.8 billion. With some confidence, we can say that consumer debt has risen because baby boomers came of age during the 1980s. To put all this in perspective, the average American carries $14,500 in consumer debt, not including mortgages, according to the Federal Reserve Board. The Credit Card Management Group, an industry association, estimates that each American adult holds two bank credit cards and another four to five retailer-issued charge cards. A two-income family conceivably could have ten different credit cards—ten different ways of borrowing money instantly. Those statistics sound dangerous, and they are; as consumer debt and credit card use soared in the 1980s, so did bad debt, rising from $601.6 million in 1980 to $3.4 billion in 1988. The federal government isn't the only one facing a major deficit in the 1990s. Total consumer debt as a percent of disposable personal income rose from 18.3 percent to 21.5 percent in 1987. Debt has become the most crippling element in our family finances, as well as in our businesses and governments; the effective elimination and management of debt is of paramount urgency.

We shouldn't waste time or energy blaming ourselves or anyone else for our crushing debt load. Our childhood environment made our credit-oriented behavior possible. Credit consumerism is a learned behavior. We now must unlearn what society has taught us so well.

America—The Land of Opportunity

Think back. Do you remember constructive conversations about the family's finances held over dinner? Or do you recall, vaguely or distinctly, not-so-pleasant conversations your parents may have had about money? Maybe you can't remember such conversations because they never happened. Among American families, money is just one of those things you don't talk about— right up there with sex, religion, and politics as a major taboo topic. You're supposed to know how to handle money; you're just not supposed to talk about it.

For children in America, financial education at home or at school is virtually nonexistent. Few schools actually provide any kind of basic education on personal finances. The one semester of economics required for graduation from California high schools since 1987, for example, is part of the history and social science curriculum. Other courses in financial matters are available through vocational business classes, but students on the collegebound track couldn't take the detour. About the closest many of us ever came to learning about personal finances was grade-school math worksheets that asked us to circle the pictures of coins amounting to fifty-nine cents. It didn't tell us what to do with the coins once we circled them, but at least we'd be able to know how much money jingled about in our pockets. Girls who would be wives were taught that boys who would be husbands would handle the family finances. Boys weren't taught anything at all. It's almost as if money management is a talent you're supposed to achieve automatically. You reach puberty, you know how to balance a checkbook and get a loan. Unfortunately, we never learned what to do with money, even after we had it.

Have It Now, Spend It Now

Americans, long considered the wealthiest people on earth, certainly aren't the wisest when it comes to family finance. We embrace a "have it now, spend it now" mentality. As the statistics we've cited point out, we save very little. The savings and loan crisis has made saving seem almost pointless. "What's the use?" we may wonder. "Insolvent thrifts are just going to lose our money for us anyway."

Baby boomers suffered the added injustice of coming of financial age during a period of high inflation—when it made far more sense to borrow money and pay it off with cheaper dollars later than to save good dollars and get rewarded with cheaper dollars. In 1980, the beginning of the post–Carter era recession, inflation was about 10 percent, mortgage rates were about 14 percent, and the passbook savings rate was 6 percent. You could get an 11.6 percent yield from a Treasury Bill, while the Standard & Poor's 500 index yielded 5.3 percent. With inflation at double-digit levels, it was actually more prudent to borrow money than to save money. Unfortunately, it was a window of opportunity that closed and then shattered on us. By 1988, Treasury Bill yields had slipped to 8.3 percent. The Standard & Poor's 500 yield dropped to 3.1 percent. And debt piled up.

Our spending habits have changed, too. The *Monthly Labor Review* has recorded data on consumer spending since 1901, and its findings are remarkable. The most amazing modification in consumer expenditures has been in housing. In 1950, when many of our parents were just starting out with young children at the beginning of the baby boom, housing represented only 10.7 percent of total income. By 1987, that figure had nearly doubled, rising to 20.2 percent. Look at it another way: housing ate up only one-tenth of our parents' incomes; it eats up at least one-fifth of ours. It's not unusual for baby boomers who bought houses in the 1980s to spend a third or more of their gross annual incomes on housing. Then consider this: the 10.7 percent figure of our parents' young adulthood was even less than what their parents had to shell out—15.1 percent of their incomes. The parents of the baby boom generation had a pretty good deal.

Food as a percentage of total expenditures declined from 34.7 percent in 1936 to 32.5 percent in 1950 to 26 percent in 1960 to 19 percent in 1987 (the most recent figures available). Food may be getting relatively cheaper, with the proliferation of grocery stores, better distribution, refrigeration, and the economical and technical efficiencies, but we're spending more of our food dollars eating out. In 1909, the first year the Bureau of Labor Statistics considered food purchased away from home, only 3 percent of the total food budget was spent on eating out. Today, 29 percent of the total food budget is spent in restaurants and at fast-food chains.

In fact, almost every aspect of the family budget has increased from 1950 to 1987: vehicle expense doubled from 12 percent to 24 percent of total income; education rose from 0.4 percent to 1 percent; utilities, fuels, and public service doubled from 4.3 percent to 8.2 percent. To be fair, some costs have actually come down. Household furnishings have dropped from 7.1 percent to 3.9 percent from 1950 to 1987. Apparel and services are down from 11.6 percent to 5.2 percent. We don't present these statistics just to depress you about the state of the economy, but to show that your financial troubles are the result of a lot of outside pressures—social and economic.

The Disposable Economy

Many Americans also have had what seems to be an innate belief that resources are unlimited, no matter what they are— oil, water, trees, opportunity. Except for native Americans, all

Americans arrived here from other lands looking for a better life, and the natural bounty of the continent fulfilled our parents' (or grandparents' or great-grandparents') dreams. Only now have we begun to realize that we do not have an infinite supply of resources. We talk about conservation just like we talk about saving money—it's a good idea, but for a little later down the road. Earth Day may have jolted consciousness about recycling; we could well use a "Finance Day" to awaken us to the idea of conserving financial resources.

Money is wasted in subtle ways. Superfluous spending is probably the most common. It is not unusual for families to have as many as four television sets, three VCRs, a couple of stereos. An average consumer might buy a new outfit, wear it once, then shove it into the back of the closet because he or she never liked the color, or the style, or gained weight after buying it.

We've been trained to buy and throw away. So many items in our culture are truly disposable: razors, diapers, cameras, even contact lenses. Appliances, once carefully maintained, are nearly disposable, too. If a toaster or an alarm clock breaks, out it goes. It's too much trouble to deal with the warranty material (if you've even kept it), find a repair shop, or pay the high labor costs associated with most repairs. Toys are disposable. So many toys have moving parts, sharp edges, limited functions. Children tire of them, or the toys break and they're either thrown away or shoved into the back of a closet.

There's even disposable equity, as real-life examples show. John and Kelly Conway could be known as Mr. and Mrs. Lifestyle. But they're also socially conscious. Their primary cause is preserving the rain forests of the Amazon; they are serious in their efforts to stop the depletion of those fragile forests. They urge conservation and self-restraint for the sake of the environment, but they haven't managed to apply the same prudence to their own lives. They're caught in a trap of wanting everything, now. They imagine that the supply of money is unlimited because of credit, and that they essentially have unlimited permission to spend money. Adding fuel to the fire burning down their own financial forest is the equity in their Southern California home. Their home's rapid appreciation has bailed them out of hip-deep debt several times. They ran their debt up to $70,000 and then refinanced their house to pay it off. The practice made sense to them because the house appreciated so rapidly and by so much that they almost felt obligated to use its value to support their lifestyle. But what do they have now? A hefty mortgage payment each month and less equity than they had ten years ago.

A more subtle factor of our throwaway economy is the games we grew up playing: Monopoly, Life, Risk. How have those games affected us? No real value is attached to cash anymore: it's play money. Beth Grandison recalled an evening out with her husband, Hal, a year before they came to see us. "We had bought tickets for a movie that had just come out. It cost us $6 each. We were running late. By the time we got to the front of the line for seats, we were pretty sure we wouldn't get good seats. The place was packed. Hal said, 'Forget it. There's no way we're going to be comfortable. Let's go. I don't care about the twelve bucks.' " Hal was ready to throw away $12 because he didn't think he'd have a good seat. Instead of arriving early to get a place near the front of the line for choice seats inside the theater, the Grandisons arrived late and then were ready to cut their losses self-indulgently. "I convinced Hal to stay, but he grumbled the whole time. And we did have pretty lousy seats," Beth said.

The willingness to kiss $12 good-bye instead of plan ahead is rampant in our society. Maybe it comes from the counter-culture resistance to authority and celebration of spontaneity, or maybe the half hour spent standing in line seems worth gambling on $12 for *potentially* bad seats. There's always a way to rationalize.

It's up to us. Just as we no longer can afford to waste water, fuel, or other natural resources, we cannot continue to waste money. Just as the 1990s will be known as the decade of the environment, so should you consider it the decade of organizing your finances. You'll breathe easier on both counts.

|||| CHECKPOINT 1 ||||

Riches don't just come in a balance sheet or in a checkbook. As many of us are finding, careers are important, money is fine, but our generation is beginning to place more value on family life and on the personal satisfaction that comes from doing what you want to do. And much of financial fulfillment has to do with attitude, perception, and communication. After each chapter, we reaffirm the key points of that chapter. We also ask you some questions that we hope you'll discuss with your spouse as you begin to communicate about your family's money and explore your own motivations and payoffs.

The baby boomer generation is the first credit-based generation in history; your struggle with debt isn't all your fault.

In this first review, we want you to think about how you regarded money during your childhood. As you discuss each question with your spouse or mull it over in your head, try to apply your answers about your youth to the way you behave today.

1. What's your first recollection of talking with your parents about money?

2. Who managed the money in your family as you were growing up?

3. What is your earliest recollection of money management? Did you have an allowance you were expected to use in a certain way: save some, spend some? What were the consequences of the way you used your allowance? Did you run out before each week's distribution? Did you have some left over?

4. Did your parents provide you with a guiding principle about money? What was it? How well did you understand what they were trying to tell you?

5. How old were you when you opened your first savings account and checking account? Whose idea was it?

6. When did you get your first credit card, and what was the credit limit? Why and how did you obtain the card?

7. What would your parents say about how you manage money?

8. How have your values and motivations regarding savings and debt changed in the last ten years, five years, three years, and the last year?

In answering these questions, what did you learn about your approach to financial matters? How much are you finding that your attitudes about money were sown in childhood experience? Allow yourself some time to just look and observe your situation rather than beat yourself over the head about it.

2

The Dynamics
of Two Incomes

T hrough the sixties and seventies, couples began to treat each other more as equals, and the subject of equality dominated public and private discussions. Traditional roles still apply for many couples, but now both spouses may take responsibility for such tasks as washing the dishes, getting the car fixed, and arranging for child care.

The evolution to equal-partner marriage may not be complete, but what's happened so far is exciting. We are good role models for our children, and maybe even for our parents. We have an enlightened family structure, in which each partner has a career that's important to himself or herself, in which children are given more of a say in what the family does, and in which members generally respect one another's identities.

Unfortunately, with this wonderful silver lining comes a cloud. And that's money. Proportionally, it's more expensive to live in the United States today than it was in the decade or two after World War II. And since the early 1970s, income has stayed relatively flat, but prices certainly have not. In 1988, the median family income was $32,191—just slightly more than

$30,084 (adjusted for inflation), the median in 1972. The same family earned the equivalent of $16,079 in 1942. No one said life is fair, but at least it's not because of a character flaw that managing finances is tough. Take some solace from that.

Our parents had the decided advantage, however offensive it may seem to our social sensibilities, of raising families in the golden economic age following World War II. It was a "Leave It to Beaver" kind of world. Dad went to work. Mom stayed home and took care of the family. Dad was the boss, at least officially. It was simple, not necessarily good or even better, but it was simple.

The two-paycheck family is common in American life today. There are more than 22 million women in the work force. The Population Research Center at the Rand Corporation predicts the number will swell to 30 million in the next decade.

Danger: Women at Work

Today's two-paycheck family is a result of two dynamics—the drive by women encouraged by the women's movement of the 1970s to achieve more than their mothers did and the increasing necessity for two incomes just to make ends meet. In 1950, only 32 percent of all women had jobs of any kind, according to the Bureau of Labor Statistics. By 1960, the figure had risen to 32.2 percent. But by 1972, the year in which the Labor Bureau first started categorizing careers, 41 percent of all women had jobs. And by 1989, the latest figures available, 54.3 percent of all women worked.

And while women still earn only about sixty-five cents for every dollar men earn, the number of women in professional fields is rising rapidly—and that means higher incomes. In 1972, only 4.6 percent of all working women held executive, administrative, or managerial jobs. By 1989, 11.1 percent of working women held those jobs—more than a twofold increase.

The number of career-minded and career-motivated women increased dramatically beginning in the late 1960s. Then in the late 1970s, women began maintaining a career even after they married and started families, a major shift from prior generations and even from the 1960s. In the late 1980s, the drain of being "superwoman" took its toll. Today's career woman often takes a full-blown maternity leave, if not a year or two off, with a new baby.

Adjusting to major shifts in traditional family roles has been difficult. As we noted in chapter 1, girls on the whole were taught, either explicitly or implicitly, that boys would run the family finances. Many baby boomer girls began to know early in their educations that they wanted careers just as much as did boys. The understanding that they would have careers was easy enough to grasp—after all, they were educated to get jobs—but the social perception that boys would take care of finances in a marriage still prevailed.

What we have found is that women climbed out of the kitchen onto the corporate ladder, but they didn't make any progress as far as finances are concerned. Two-income families face the added complication of problems that are peculiar to their condition. Two-income families aren't just two one-income families combined. The questions and dilemmas have multiplied exponentially and range from the emotional to the practical.

When *Money* magazine asked, "What's more important in your life—sex or money?" 24 percent of the two-income families polled responded *sex*. Thirty-seven percent answered *money*. Of all the new problems baffling and disturbing the nation's two-paycheck families, money looms largest.

The Extra Costs of Two-Income Couples

One of the problems of two-paycheck living is that the costs are not all on the table. Hidden extra costs can be so formidable that they can wipe out the benefit of the second income and turn one spouse's job into a liability. Fortunately, recognizing and coping with the extra costs is the first step to sane financial planning—one key to setting family goals. Unfortunately, the answer isn't as simple as having the second-income spouse quit work and stay home, although that may be one of the options to consider. Today's two-*paycheck* families are often two-*career* families, and working usually means self-fulfillment for both spouses.

Nevertheless, much can be done about extra costs if they are clearly and honestly examined. Although it may seem that clothing, restaurant meals, and so on would be the same whether the individuals lived together or apart, we've found that almost without exception, couples who spend together tend to spend more than they would as individuals.

The Extra Costs of the Second Job

Clothing: Even in bare necessities, such as clothing and accessories, sending two people to work every day costs more than sending one. No matter how liberal some companies are, such as computer companies that encourage employees to report for work in jeans and sneakers, most jobs require that you fit the company image. You're expected to look as good as your CEO, on a much smaller salary.

Food: A second job also means more meals eaten outside the home. If two people have to get ready for work in the morning, sack lunches generally won't get packed.

Laundry and Cleaning: Most of those imitation-CEO suits have to be dry-cleaned, and suddenly it makes much more sense to send shirts and blouses to the laundry, too. And weekends are made for R & R, not scrubbing floors. Cleaning services are another extra cost.

Transportation: Don't forget commuting costs. In the San Francisco Bay area, where most of our clients live, mass transportation costs anywhere from $3 to $10 roundtrip—or as much as $735 to $2,450 a year. If you have to drive, pay tolls, and park, you're looking at easily more than $2,500 a year.

Taxes: Of course the real kick in the pants is from everyone's favorite uncle—the U.S. government. If one spouse earns $50,000 and the other earns $30,000, they're obviously taxed as an $80,000 household. However, that means the $30,000 income is getting taxed at a much higher rate than if the individual were single and earning $30,000. Essentially, taxes are higher if you're married. Being thrust into a higher tax bracket with a second income can even erode much of that second, lower income. All of this may seem like mere pocket money, but it's not. The U.S. Department of Health and Human Services estimates that the costs of holding a job total about 32 percent of gross salary.

The Extra Costs of Raising Kids

Anyone who's handed five dollars to a child to buy lunch knows that it costs more to have children when you both have careers. With time at a premium, it's easier to send a teenage daughter to buy clothes "on the card" than it is to accompany her to the store and monitor spending. We've found that many parents also attempt to compensate for lack of quality time, perceived or actual, with their children by buying the kids the latest in leather sneakers, videogames, music, and clothing, even though they know what the experts know: material goods don't necessarily make kids happier, though kids would like you to believe otherwise. With small children, the overriding cost is child care. In some major metropolitan areas, the cost of good child care can almost obliterate the income from some jobs.

A relatively new phenomenon we've encountered is children who have some actual say in how the family spends its money because the parents don't always have the time: children who make purchasing decisions, not just influence them, constitute a multibillion-dollar market. Financing education also is a huge part of the extra costs of having kids in a two-income family. The Rand Institute has found that college is a cultural necessity for children in eight out of ten two-paycheck families, compared with two out of ten one-paycheck families.

The National Institutes of Health estimates that a two-paycheck family earning $65,000 a year will spend about $400,000 on their two kids by the time the kids are eighteen—about $120,000 more than a one-paycheck family with the *same* income.

The Extra Costs of Financial "Rights"

In the old days, financial "rights" were not a significant issue. One paycheck came in and everyone's needs were met from that one source. Now, with two-career, two-income couples, many other variables determine how the money is ultimately spent. Some couples separate their funds entirely; some hold certain assets jointly, such as real estate or savings. But with these variations, who pays for what? How is the mortgage split? Who's responsible for the utilities bills? What if one spouse has a primary job and then does consulting on the side—is the extra money communal? Can the person who makes more spend more on toys for himself or herself? Does the spouse who makes less feel uncomfortable taking lavish vacations or going to expensive restaurants? For that matter, how do you even go about deciding? Does someone have final say? If all these questions go unanswered, the result can be financial chaos and wasteful spending. Without communicating, spouses tend to spend as if they were single, with no real regard for the family's bottom line.

The Extra Costs of the Illusion of Affluence

Many two-income couples live in the blissful belief that they have as much as three times the amount of money they actually have. After all, we make three times the salary that our parents did. And, in many cases, two-income couples, believing that they have to show the world how well they've succeeded, spend extravagantly—with the help of credit.

Real-life Dilemmas

The sum of these extra costs can be staggering. For Tim and Jill Gladden, who came to us to help them sort out their financial maze, a typical two-paycheck, two-kids family grossing $65,000 a year, the costs added up to about $20,000. The Gladdens have about $50,000 of their $65,000 joint income to spend after taxes. Or so they think. But the extra costs of the second job, the kids, and the lack of organization cuts that $50,000 to $37,000. But, like most of us who don't really want to know what the bottom line is, the Gladdens continued to spend as though they still had $50,000 after taxes. Because of this misconception, they piled up $13,000 in debt a year.

Jill and Tim were intensely proud of their teenage sons, Chad and Terry. The boys were the stuff of All-American heroes. They excelled in academics, sports, and community service. They charmed everyone they met, and yet they were modest enough not to be obnoxious. Jill and Tim's spending habits reflected their pride. The couple wanted their sons to have everything they needed to continue their successes; they didn't consider their purchases as superfluous. Their boys were talented, and the couple wanted to give them the tools they needed to excel.

Chad and Terry were addicted to sports: rugby, lacrosse, baseball, water polo, everything. And their parents provided the equipment for each new sport the boys discovered. They also did well in school, so their parents paid for private college counselors and SAT preparation courses. Their community service—Chad worked at the hospital as a volunteer and Terry coached a youth soccer team—took up a lot of time, too. With all their activities, they didn't have time for part-time jobs.

The Gladdens aren't spendthrifts. In fact, they have a policy of discussing major expenditures before making them. Jill recalled when Tim wanted to buy a new television. The boys were watching so much ESPN—soccer, fencing, wrestling, golf, basketball, volleyball, powerlifting, bodybuilding, flyfishing—that Tim and Jill only occasionally were able to settle in to a movie and be cozy. The couple decided, after years of resisting, to buy a television for the bedroom, preferably one just as nice as that in the family room. They knew they could afford it by using their credit card. The set Tim wanted cost $700.

"We always felt good about our policy of discussing major expenditures—some of our friends just go out and buy without talking about it. But our discussions often turned into mutual encouragement sessions, collective rationalization," Jill said. "What we should have done is told the boys that if they were going to watch so much television, they should find a way to buy a set themselves. But it was easier to take care of the situation ourselves. Tim and I have good jobs and sometimes I feel a little guilty about not being a 'traditional' mom, whatever that is, so we bought the $700 television, which we don't watch very often."

Like the Gladdens, the Belkins are in a similar bind. Robert and Katherine Belkin are another working couple who thoroughly enjoy their family. When we started working with them, we saw right away that their family was the focus of their lives. From their enthusiasm for both their family and their careers, it's obvious they made the right choice in launching both simultaneously, but without any formal approach to financial management, the Belkins have run into some serious problems.

"Where does it all go?" a perplexed Katherine asked us.

The Belkins, busy with their two careers, give their children, ages nine and twelve, some spending leeway and responsibilities. The Belkin kids even plan family menus. "They get to decide pretty much what goes on the grocery list. They bring home the most expensive items. They don't comparison shop, but who has the time to handle the shopping? I figure it's a tradeoff."

For the Belkins, it turned out to be a very expensive tradeoff. From what we've found with the Belkins and other couples, having children make purchasing decisions creates extra costs averaging about 2 percent of joint take-home pay. The extra cost for the Belkins added up to 3 percent of their joint pay.

Robert pointed out that the kids recently needed new sneakers. He didn't have time to take them shopping, so he gave them his credit card and told them not to spend more than $50 each. When he got the bill, he saw they'd each spent $80, but what could he say? "Yeah, if I'd taken them, I'd have saved $60."

The fact is that busy lives cost more. It's easy to fool yourself by saying, "I'm working twelve hours a day, spending quality time with the kids, and taking care of the house. I don't have extra costs; I don't have time to spend any money."

The reality is that when you do spend, whether it's dinner out because you worked late or it's a new pair of athletic shoes because you had a hard week and you deserve them, you're probably spending more than you would otherwise. It's very easy to spend money as a way of relaxing, of playing. And when two people work, you feel a certain sense of freedom. You assume you can afford whatever you want. Often, as the Gladdens discovered, you give each other permission to overspend, bending over backwards not to censor—lest it be done unto you. Single people likely would have said, "I really like that $700 television. But I can't afford it. I think I'll buy this $400 set." No one says to the single person, "We work hard, we deserve the other one."

What we want you to consider is this: What do you really want? In the next chapter we're going to try to figure out how you really feel about money and its effect on your family.

‖‖‖ CHECKPOINT 2 ‖‖‖

A two-income family is a modern structure in which family members share more responsibilities and respect.

Without guidance, the financial side can get out of control as you are faced with the extra costs of being a two-income family—from spending money on the kids to make up for lack of quality time to eating out frequently because you're too tired to cook.

You have the capability to create a healthy financial life.

1. Women: When did you decide or realize that you would have a career?

2. Women: How has having a career affected your relationship to money? Compare your attitude and practices to those of your mother, whether she was a career woman or not. How are you different? The same?

3. Men: When did you realize that in all likelihood your spouse would be a career woman? Compare your attitude and practices about money to those of your father. How are you different? The same?

4. Do you perceive the extra costs of having a second job? Why does your family have a second job—for reasons of personal fulfillment or of financial necessity?

5. Would you be a two-income family if you had the option? Supposing you wanted to be a one-income family, who would work and why? What would the person staying home do?

6. How often do you give your children a credit card to make purchases? When was the last time, and what was your feeling when your children arrived home with their purchases?

7. Do you feel you have more spending power with two incomes than you had with one, or than you had as a single person?

8. As a couple and as individuals, how well defined are your financial rights? Do you have any formal agreement on how money is spent? Who makes the financial decisions?

3

How Do You Feel About Money?

e've all heard the phrase "Why worry about a little thing like money?" We've all said it facetiously when we're faced with a gigantic bill for something like insurance; cavalierly when we want to go to the Caribbean and can't afford it; and seriously when we were idealistic youths flirting with socialism.

But people do worry about money, and the emotions that accompany the worry range from confidence to desperation. Many people

- Are upset with, uncomfortable about, or frustrated by their cash flow situation
- Take action only when the situation becomes unbearable
- Are motivated by desperation, not a quest for success
- Have an abiding feeling that they can lose everything

Emotions dominate our behavior more often than we are willing to admit. When the topic of money arises, many people think they can—and should—approach it rationally, even dispassionately. But most people are *directed to* or *directed from* any given circumstance, even one relating to money: people run toward things or feelings they want; they run from things or feelings they don't want or that make them uncomfortable. Pinpointing the feelings and conditions that you are most eager to achieve is one of the important aspects of addressing your own financial situation. Ultimately, the energy of your likes and desires will propel you toward your goals.

Bob and Cathy Leigh were both high-powered corporate attorneys whose days were filled with conflict and resolution as they battled in court. Both were used to knowing exactly what they wanted and making decisions quickly as they charged toward their goal: winning the case. But they were unable to apply the same energy toward their own financial condition, which was shaky. By confronting their feelings about money and identifying their desires, the Leighs were able to take charge of their finances and set goals. Often, people can't take action because they don't understand the forces behind their behavior.

Here's a list of the emotions our clients most commonly express when they come to us for help:

hopelessness	frustration
anger	helplessness
embarrassment	vulnerability
oppression	anxiety
fear	resentment
guilt	bitterness
turmoil	

People turn the tide of upset when they begin to

- Talk with their spouse about their feelings
- Clearly identify their goals
- Chart a course of action
- Take positive steps toward their goals
- Pay bills on time

- Save money
- Reduce debt

When they've wrested control of their financial life and claimed it for themselves, they experience a new set of feelings:

empowerment	direction
contentment	determination
accomplishment	composure
proficiency	security
self-confidence	assurance

It is one thing to face financial problems when you're single, but in a partnership, you have to confront and determine your common or disparate goals and compromise when you have different ideas and dreams. (We discuss mutual goals versus individual desires in chapter 8.) Kevin and Kim Perry are a prime example of the unexpected benefits—both individual and joint—of taking control of their financial condition. Kevin, a dentist, loved music. To relax after work and express what Kim called "his feminine, sensitive side," Kevin spent an hour each evening at the piano. He had often dreamed of having a mini-studio in which he could record and orchestrate his compositions. Kim, a stockbroker, loved horses and had always dreamed about taking an equestrian tour of Ireland. When they discussed these dreams, they either spoke in the past tense ("as in ancient history, or 'dream on,' " Kevin said) or treated the dreams as pleasant but unachievable fantasies. They weren't common goals, so the Perrys put them aside.

Their common goal was to buy a house before they were thirty-five. At thirty-three, they had come nowhere close to achieving that goal, and they began to express their disappointment in their spending habits. They spent a little here and there on household luxuries they could both agree on, a couple of short vacations, and never addressed the real issue of buying a house. They often griped about their individual fantasies and resented each other's dreams. When they finally reidentified their common goal—buying a house—they also found they were more comfortable about discussing their individual dreams. Within a few years, by focusing on their shared dreams, they had the house they wanted, Kevin had acquired an electronic keyboard as his first step toward recognizing his dream, and Kim had opened a savings account for her Ireland horseback tour.

Are You Communicating?

Remember dating? The glow of preparing for a date, deciding where to go, what to wear, what to say. You worked up to it all week long, whether the invitation was "I'd like to take you to dinner and a movie Saturday night" or "Doing anything Saturday?" Dates were special—it didn't matter really what you did or where you went. You were with a special person, and you knew you'd have fun. And, if you didn't, you'd still have something to talk about at work on Monday.

What was magical about most dates was the lack of concern about money. You were always able to scrape up enough for a date. Even if your date ran short, you always had some—at least enough to get through a Saturday night, including drinks at a bar or ice cream later. One of you could always supplement. If you spent too much one weekend, you could get by with the old peanut-butter diet. Sometimes, as dating got more serious, there were little gifts. Maybe flowers, maybe a trinket for the bookshelf. And when money was scarce, that didn't matter either. You just had a good time being together. Not having much money could even be romantic; you could laugh about it. You probably never discussed money, except in vaguest terms. It wasn't romantic and seemed to serve no purpose anyway. Who cared? You were out to have a good time. When you date, you are a little afraid to show your true feelings about money. It is impolite to pry. We were taught that one doesn't discuss money in polite company.

And yes, there is a *but* to this story. When you got married, suddenly you had to deal with money, to sort our your feelings about money, and to combine your finances. China patterns are easier to mix than checkbooks. You didn't bicker about money before you got married, because everything was separate and your girlfriend's or boyfriend's finances really were none of your business. Once you marry, the steady date is your wife or husband and it *is* your business. Suddenly, the way you feel about money is somebody else's business, too.

Money is an emotional subject, even when you're single. When two people who have different upbringings and experiences with money try to combine every aspect of their financial lives, from grandma's jewelry to the groceries, the potential for upset is dramatically increased. Two-income families have a fundamental struggle about money that single-income families just don't experience. If one spouse is working, the other naturally defers some of the decision-making authority, regardless of any preset notion of sharing every decision. Quite simply, even if you're raising the kids, composing music, writing a book, painting, in training for a grueling athletic event, or going to school—there's something in you that regards the family breadwinner as the decision maker. But if two people are earning the money, usually either no one defers or the person who does resents the decision maker's power. Even when neither spouse defers and decisions are made jointly, problems can arise. Sometimes sharing an attitude can lead to trouble, as it did with the Gladdens, who easily talked themselves into the $700 television they could not really afford.

Merely recognizing the problem isn't enough. The Carmines came to us deep in debt, with a taste for expensive accoutrements. They liked their lifestyle, but their discomfort over the debt was beginning to get in the way. Like our other clients who came to us for direction, the Carmines began to chart a course toward eradicating their debt. We handled their checkbook, paid their bills, and helped them determine their common goals. Still, despite the best of intentions, they had trouble understanding the process. They went through all the proper procedures, but they never "got it." It was clear that, like binge eaters, they would go back to their old habits once this annoying "diet" ended.

Carl Carmine couldn't bear the thought of his wife, Donna, spending any money if he didn't think he would have the same amount to spend, almost immediately. The Carmines individually had the authority to request a check drawn from their discretionary account with us. Carl called us repeatedly: "Whenever my wife gets a check from you, I want you to cut me a check for the same amount." He thought she wasted money, and he wanted to be able to waste just as much. Fundamentally, Carl and Donna didn't understand or discuss each other's feelings about money. Although we had assumed responsibility for their bills, thus removing one of the problems, they still managed to evade the underlying issue. Just surrendering control of their cash flow couldn't heal the deeper wound. Over time they found that their common goals provided a foundation for reestablishing trust and working out their competitive differences.

One of two dynamics influences most two-income families' approach to their finances. Either the couple share similar spending and saving patterns or they don't. Either way, once you settle into an emotional spending pattern as a couple, it shapes the way you relate to each other—both in constructive and troublesome ways. But you can change, as we'll demonstrate in chapters 6 and 7, by focusing on common goals.

Partners in two-income families also face the issue of promoting their individual careers. In the old days, Dad brought the boss home for dinner, and Mom cooked and served as a perfect hostess. The kids dutifully went along to company picnics. Dad's career was paramount because it fed everybody. Two-income couples are faced with balancing their careers and sharing the spousal "requirements," such as enduring the other spouse's boss even if you think he's a bigot. On top of that, we often feel the need to project the right image—to send a message to the world about the lifestyle and professional status to which we aspire.

Dale and Julie Harberger love their careers, so much so that they are willing to make some sacrifices in their private lives, which are, in turn, inextricably intertwined with their careers. Dale is a commercial real estate broker for a small brokerage firm that had just been acquired by a large Japanese company. Julie is an attorney with a midsize law firm. Image is very important to them, which they readily admit. They wanted a big house that would reflect and magnify their positions. They couldn't really afford the house they bought, but they figured their incomes would enjoy double-digit annual increases and the value of the house would appreciate over time as well. They knew they wouldn't be taking any lavish vacations, but they really wanted the house. After they moved in, they began to fill their new home with contemporary art and contemporary furniture that could double as art—all expensive. Julie had a library that Winston Churchill would have envied. She had always wanted a grand library with floor-to-ceiling mahogany bookshelves, hardwood floors, a partner's desk, and a leather oxblood executive's chair. Dale had transformed the basement into a weight room with the best fitness equipment credit could buy. Together, they love to entertain and feel that their careers depend upon it. Getting ahead means meeting with the right people as often as possible.

As a result, Dale and Julie don't have a dime. They have no savings. Last Christmas they had a blowout catered party to which they invited their bosses and friends. They considered it an investment in their future. But as they began to communicate, they realized they'd tacitly given each other permission to spend beyond their combined means. "I felt I needed to impress the partners and get them to see that I am partner material, an image to augment my abilities as an attorney. Dale agreed with me. He wanted to do the same thing," Julie said. Dale chimed in, "I was doing fine with my firm before the acquisition. Now instead of working for a small firm with lots of potential, I'm working for a conglomerate and am not as noticeable. So, I felt I had to show off a bit. The commercial real estate business is a lot of flash and glitz and game-playing." Together, they'd been feeding the flames of debt.

If by now you've recognized that you and your spouse have failed to communicate clearly about money, you have probably also realized that you're not alone. No matter how much you get paid, no matter where you went to school or what kind of car you drive, you can fall into the trap of spending more than you make. What does matter is that you've somehow forgotten your common goals, or you failed to set them in the first place. Those goals are important, and we want you to realize them.

Liz Davis first came to us three years ago, a successful single woman who nevertheless wasn't very happy with her life or her career. She had always wanted to go to art school. But to compensate for feeling unhappy at her job as a loan officer, Liz went shopping at lunchtime, often spending as much as $50 in a one-hour break—every day. That's $250 a week, or $1,000 a month. Liz's $25,000 annual salary couldn't support that kind of spending. She came to us with $10,000 in consumer debt and the realization that she needed someone else to take control of her finances or she'd drown in a sea of debt, even as her creditors were trying to convince her that she could swim like a financial champion.

We helped Liz sort out her feelings about money and begin to pay off her debt. She sustained her effort and realized her dream of attending art school at night by significantly reducing her weekday spending. She found a new job at a corporate art consulting firm, which didn't pay as much but made her much happier. She had achieved most of her goals, which had become obscured by her day-to-day drive to disguise her unhappiness. She had begun to feel very good about her spending habits and to treat money as a tool for achieving her goals rather than a tourniquet for discontent.

Then she met Max Carberry. Max was a friend's husband's old roommate. A news editor, Max talked about world events with the authority and skepticism of a journalist. He respected Liz's opinion and they enjoyed lively debates on a wide array of topics. But there was at least one warning light that Liz ignored as they took off into a turbocharged romance. "He has more credit cards than anyone I ever met," Liz's best friend had described Max, laughing. The problem was that Max was in the same situation Liz had been in two years before—with goals askew and finances in a state of disaster. Max did have a portfolio of credit cards—most of them were run up to the limit. He had a fancy car, complete with car payments. He had an unbelievable stereo system, which he'd financed. He had a personal line of credit that sent him to Tahiti the year before, with another girlfriend. And, as it turned out, he had borrowed to raise the money for the trip he and Liz took to Australia.

In short, Max was living in a rock-and-roll world. He loved to play, and he loved to make people happy with his footloose attitude. Liz thoroughly enjoyed being with him, but the ecstasy of romance disguised the reality of Max's approach to money. While Max and Liz were dating, life was glorious. Because she had been in the same position, Liz was understanding and compassionate about his situation, and she remained comfortable and confident about her own finances because she had finally achieved a healthy relationship with money.

Once they married and combined their finances, life was still glorious because Liz and Max were madly in love. But Liz's financial confidence began to erode. Because Max admired the way Liz had taken control of her money, he turned over his finances for her to manage. She was pleased to help, but the enormity of his troubles began to worry her. Collection notices for debts Max had just "forgotten about" began to arrive. She discovered that he'd neglected to file a $5,000 expense report for a business trip. Almost overnight, she absorbed his emotions about money. She was no longer comfortable, confident Liz Davis. Once again, she had begun experiencing the gnawing discomfort of an overwhelming task. Liz came back to us, this time with Max, to address the problem and set up a plan they could mutually act on.

Liz and Max are like many other couples whose financial practices can be as dissimilar as a husband who likes the Rolling Stones and a wife who likes Puccini. When we have nothing at stake in another person's financial behavior, we naturally ignore our concerns about their troubles. Once we're married, their troubles are ours. The forgotten expense report is $5,000 of mutual debt—which doesn't mean it's half as bad.

What's Missing?

Generally, it's not the actual money that's the trouble—it's what the money does or doesn't achieve for you that satisfies or frustrates you. Most of us have probably studied our combined incomes and said, "We make $80,000 a year. Where does it all go and how come we're not living lives that reflect that kind of income? We didn't even go on vacation last year!"

Vacation is a good example. We might say: "We never take a vacation," but what's actually missing isn't the vacation itself, but the joy, the comfort, the relaxation, the element of renewed vigor that comes from taking a vacation. What prevents us is the debt we've acquired pursuing our lifestyle with no regard to planning for the things, such as the psychological release of a vacation, that we really want and need.

One of our clients lamented, "Before I got married, I had only a sports car. Now that I'm married, I still have only a sports car, and, somehow, $14,000 in debt." The trouble is that when you get married, you start building a new life together. You sit down to dinner together, so you need dishes, furniture, and appliances. The initial setting up of a household was probably funded at least in part by monetary wedding gifts. But the purchases didn't stop after the gifts ran out. After five to ten years of marriage, your values may still be the same, but you're drifting. It's easy to get complacent, but how do you get back on track?

In short, dreams and goals. If you're both working toward the same goal, a dynamic begins to develop that makes achieving it more real. Ease up on the drudgery of economics. Don't make your goals solely academic, like reducing debt. Learn to dream together. When you're both participating, you'll experience a vibrancy and liveliness that may have diminished along the way. We're talking about rekindling the relationship. Money can't buy happiness, but taking control of your money can.

Are You Doing What You Really Want to Do?

While we're on the subject of happiness, we should address your careers. Plenty of books encourage you to do what you want, so we won't get carried away here. But what we will look at is the financial repercussions or requirements of your current situation.

Pure fantasy is easy—as in "If I could do anything I wanted to do, I'd spend a year training for an attack on Everest and then do it." Or "I think I'll wait tables at night and spend my days reading and writing." But those aspirations often aren't realistic. As a two-income family you've built yourselves into a lifestyle, you have families, you have your careers. Sometimes you feel trapped, and sometimes you resent your spouse, who is doing more of what she or he wants to do, making a little less money than you are but appearing a lot happier. We know one couple with tremendously different careers. Theo Allston is a brand manager for a large consumer-products company. His wife, Susan Miller, is a free-lance photographer. Theo makes more money and is on the inside fast track, but he leaves the house at seven at the latest each morning to arrive at work by eight, if not earlier. He leaves at five, getting home at six or six-thirty. Susan works day to day. She gets to cover exciting events, meet famous people, and control her time and work load. She can sleep late, work out leisurely at the gym after the morning rush, and then go out on a shoot.

Theo sees Susan's job as more exciting than his own, and he knows she loves what she does. Sometimes that irritates him. It's not that he doesn't like what he does, but he doesn't feel the passion for his job that he sees in Susan. He experiences bouts of resentment for Susan's job. Susan agrees that she loves what she does, but it's not always glamour and glitz. There are days when she shoots gadgets and hardware for supply catalogs, or days when she doesn't work at all. While Theo resents what he perceives as her leisure time, Susan emphasizes that she often has to use that time, unpaid and anxious, to hustle for new work, not exactly a relaxing activity. She sees Theo's job as secure, and therefore less stressful than her own. Sometimes she resents Theo's paid vacation and other benefits, such as medical insurance. Yes, she's entitled to those benefits as a spouse, but it irks her that she is dependent on his job for medical care. If she were single, she'd have to come up with coverage on her own. As it is, when she takes a vacation, she doesn't get paid.

Susan may be doing what she loves, but Theo never said when he was a kid, "Hey, I want to be a brand manager when I grow up." Theo wanted to be a pilot, a dream dashed in college when he had to quit the air force ROTC because his eyesight had started to slip and he knew he'd never fly fighters.

Through discussions and reevaluations of their goals—security and financial independence—Theo and Susan have taken control of their financial lives and begun to achieve what they really want. By eliminating their debt and by building savings, Theo has been able to start flying lessons. And because he has four weeks' vacation and Susan has only what she feels she can afford, the two agreed that Theo could spend a couple of weeks flying on his own. He hopes to start a small courier business someday. In the meantime, he expects to volunteer to transport physicians to a children's medical clinic on the Mexican border, which he figures is more useful than being a fighter pilot, anyway. Susan, on the other hand, wanted to feel more secure about her own financial condition, so the couple established savings accounts that would buoy them in the event of financial emergencies.

Too many people cling to the corporate ladder for security because they've built up a lot of debt and because they feel that's what society expects of them. But if you take control of your money, you'll be amazed at what you can accomplish.

CHECKPOINT 3

Emotions affect your financial behavior. Understanding the way you feel about money and the way you want to feel will help you chart a course of action.

1. How often do you and your spouse discuss expenditures? Do you review your finances together?

2. How often do you and your spouse argue about money? What was the last argument you had? How did you resolve it?

3. Define your spouse's values and attitudes about money on a separate sheet of paper, privately, and then compare them. What did you discover about your spouse's opinion of your attitudes?

4. What feelings do you desire from your financial condition?

5. What action are you taking to realize these feelings?

6. When you have a financial problem, do you look for a remedy? Or do you go out and spend money?

7. Are you communicating more or less about money than when you were first married? Perhaps you started out with a clear picture of what you wanted to accomplish and how you wanted to manage money. What happened?

8. People are motivated in two directions—either *away* from things they don't like or want to change or *toward* things and feelings they desire. In the appendix you will find the Primary Motivations and Payoffs chart, which you should fill out to determine what motivates you. The lower portion of the form, relating to goals, will be filled out in chapter 4.

8a. What feelings and emotions do you have about money that you want to eliminate? (Enter these answers on your Primary Motivations and Payoffs chart.)

8b. How would you like to feel about your money? (Enter these answers on your chart.)

9a. Circle the emotions and feelings that you most wish to eliminate from this list:

hopelessness	frustration
anger	helplessness
embarrassment	vulnerability
oppression	anxiety
fear	resentment
guilt	bitterness
turmoil	

Discuss what you believe causes these emotions and why you may have circled different words than your spouse circled.

9b. Circle the emotions and feelings that you most desire from this list:

empowerment	direction
contentment	determination
accomplishment	composure
proficiency	security
self-confidence	assurance

Discuss what these words mean to each of you. Perhaps you will also uncover other feelings you wish to eliminate.

4

Identifying Your Dreams

om and Lori Stack had been married ten years and had accumulated all the trappings of the Good Life. They drove sports cars, owned a four-bedroom Tudor-style home, collected artwork by rising young artists, cooked in a gourmet-equipped kitchen, listened to their new collection of compact discs, and enjoyed other symbols of success. But they also had managed to get themselves into a fair amount of debt and couldn't figure out how to eradicate it. No sooner had they managed to reduce the level of debt, when it crept up on them again. Unexpected events—from weddings to car repairs—always seemed to bash a big hole in their budget.

Making about $90,000 a year ($60,000 after taxes) between the two of them, they had enough income for the Good Life. Their total credit card debt was about $12,000, but they made the monthly minimum payments without much trouble. What finally hit Lori one day as she drove home from work was that they weren't making any headway. When she thought about it, she realized that her recollection of goals she and Tom had set before they married was only hazy. She wondered what Tom thought. Over dinner—at a restaurant and on a credit card, she recounted later with an embarrassed grin—they discussed getting their financial lives in order.

The $12,000 in debt was a lot, but it wasn't staggering. What was troublesome was their state of mind. The Stacks were a successful couple in their early thirties who felt unfulfilled. They had material possessions, but they felt cut adrift in a meaningless lifestyle sea. They were doubly frustrated because they couldn't understand their discomfort. Their ship had come in by the world's standards, but they felt the wind was no longer in their sails.

Whether they should ever have married in the first place was not an issue. It was clear in the looks they gave each other and their gentle touches that Lori and Tom loved each other very much. In the course of setting out their balance sheet and uncovering their concerns, we discovered that what Tom and Lori wanted more than anything was to start a family. But they hadn't begun to talk about that dream as a real probability. They were so busy living their lives and building their lifestyle that they'd put aside the dream they had discussed during their courtship: to have children. The truth of it was that as much as they wanted children, they were afraid to raise the subject. They were ready to have children, but in an abstract sort of way. Of course, Tom and Lori knew that having a child wasn't going to solve their financial concerns; in fact, their debt load made having a child a fiscal as well as emotional question. They realized they would have to get their finances in order to be able to afford a child.

That was the understanding they needed to reverse their financial course. Nothing anyone says about your finances is going to compel you to make a change, but once you are motivated by something you really want—something more meaningful than a clean balance sheet—you'll buckle down and get to work.

Tom and Lori had felt so overwhelmed by debt that the goal of having children became more remote and almost impossible to imagine. They had never wanted to have children immediately, but they had never set a deadline for starting their family. When Tom and Lori started again to talk about having a baby, they were motivated to control their spending and start eliminating debt. Once underway, they couldn't do it fast enough. Watching them rekindle their dream was exciting. The first hurdle had been cleared. That's when we started to talk to them about the difference between first- and second-degree desires.

Primary Versus Secondary Goals

The Stacks' primary goal, becoming parents, had been overshadowed by secondary goals—such as buying a house. Primary goals are often the very dreams that sound impractical to family and friends, but that are part of the way you define yourself. Secondary goals are those that seem almost necessary to everyday existence, but that have no other meaning beyond their immediacy. No matter how successful you are at meeting secondary goals, you will almost always feel unsatisfied because you have ignored your primary goals.

A country club membership is a sad substitute for cycling across America if a cross-country bike trip is the one thing you have wanted to do since you were ten years old. Suppressing your primary goals foments tension and conflict in your marriage. What do you do about it? Most people either spend money because they are depressed or spend money on secondary and tertiary goals because they assume they will never achieve their first desire.

Once we had determined the Stacks' motivation for getting their finances under control, we could start forming a plan for them. Our enthusiasm provided external validation for their primary goal, which they had set aside because of peer pressure (most of their friends were postponing children or swearing off becoming parents completely) and the immediacy of secondary goals.

With their $90,000 pretax income ($60,000 after tax) and $12,000 debt, we worked out a plan for them to pay off their debt at a rate of $500 a month and save for the baby at a rate of $500 a month. By the end of thirty-six months, they would have paid off the debt and have $12,000 in cash to decorate a nursery, start a college education fund, and buy video equipment to chronicle their plunge into parenthood. With renewed vision, Tom and Lori were willing to change their attitudes and spending habits in order to achieve their dream. They automatically put aside the $1,000 a month in debt reduction and savings and then considered their spending. They stopped eating out as much and buying as much for the house because the cash wasn't available. Instead, they took time to think about and plan for the new baby.

For the Stacks, debt had piled up and dreams had slipped farther away, in part because they yielded to the opinion of others.

The Perils of Peer Pressure

Much as we might like to believe that we are too sophisticated to be swayed by peer pressure—the old "keeping up with the Joneses"—we are all vulnerable to what our friends and colleagues think of us. Peer pressure entices us to buy meaningless luxuries and fad accessories, as the desire to impress overwhelms the rational perspective on spending. You are far more likely to buy a new sofa because it impresses people than tie up the same amount in a savings account toward a month-long vacation.

Karen and Alan Weiss, who lived in a region cursed with extraordinarily high home prices, needed high incomes and a fat down payment to buy the house they wanted. Karen earned $45,000 as a researcher at an investigation firm; Alan earned $60,000 as an engineer. The house they wanted would carry a monthly mortgage of $3,500. Compared to that sum, the $40,000 in cash they needed to put down was terrifying. With a healthy $2,200 a month going for rent on a large apartment in a posh part of the city, the Weisses were overwhelmed by the magnitude of the savings plan they would have to implement to buy a house. In addition, they felt they had nothing to show for their $105,000 annual income and felt a little foolish next to friends who made less but had more.

So they bought a sports car.

The car was pearly metallic white and streaked down the freeway. It was sleek and sensual and gave them a rush as they zipped around tight curves, hugging the road. Friends drooled. The Weisses shelled out $500 a month in car payments. They *did* need a new car. Karen's car was still in good shape, but Alan's car had 110,000 miles on it, and he drove a lot. Yes, he needed a car, but he didn't *have* to buy the sports car. He bought it because its image corresponded to the family income and made him feel good.

The Weisses are an example of the twin perils of peer pressure and immediate gratification. When they sacrifice their primary goals, couples go after the cheap thrills and quick-fix rewards of their secondary goals. The secondary goals, like needing a new car, tend to loom larger than the primary goals. If you have an apartment, buying a house doesn't seem all-important when the car you need to get you to work every day gives up the ghost.

For the Weisses, buying a sports car accomplished a secondary goal and alleviated some of the disappointment of not having achieved their primary goal of buying a house. But in buying a car with monthly payments of $500 instead of one with payments of $300, the Weisses forfeited $200 a month ($12,000 over five years!) they could have been saving toward the new house.

We helped the Weisses see that buying a house was possible, and recommended they start building a savings account immediately. To do this, they sold the sports car and bought a car that required lower monthly payments. Although they felt a bit chagrined about the car, they began to recognize the satisfaction of making regular deposits to savings—deposits that brought them steadily closer to their goal. Incentive, as well as building healthy habits, is important.

Everyone Needs a Reward

In starting new habits, couples need some rewards along the way. That's why we said at the beginning of this book that we wouldn't ask you to cut up your credit cards. That kind of stoicism wears off quickly and sends even the most goal-driven couple back to their old habits. For the Stacks, the reward of eradicating their debt was watching the baby account grow as quickly as the debt diminished; the Weisses watched the frame of their house go up as the prison of their debt was razed.

Whether your primary goal is early retirement, buying a house, or disappearing for a six-month world tour, you need to take time to dream about it. Secondary goals often get moved up to replace primary goals because of the chaos and preoccupation of daily life. It may sound trite or melodramatic, but it is important to remember and nurture your dreams—and to reaffirm that these goals are *your* dreams. They don't need to be validated by any third party, nor can any third party make your dreams real.

We believe, as do many financial experts, that setting goals—clarifying exactly what you want your money to do for you and your family—is the strongest motivation for pursuing and sticking with a sound cash flow management program. The dream could be the ultimate car, a trip around the world, a business of your own, going back to school, a second house, enough capital to play the stock market, or security in retirement. Identifying your dreams does take time, but daydreaming is not only a pleasant way to pass the time; it is essential for designing a fulfilling life.

Cutting back on spending or following the cash flow plan never excited the Stacks or the Weisses. Having a baby and buying a house were the thrills. Taking charge of the decisions you make benefits your psychological and financial well-being. In the next chapter you'll learn how to put your plan into action and not live by default.

⫴ CHECKPOINT 4 ⫴

Secondary goals often supersede primary goals, but by taking time to dream and by using your dream to compel you, you can realize your primary goals and get your financial life in order.

Think about the motivation behind your spending habits and reevaluate your family's goals—both financial and lifestyle.

1. "What's Our Dream?" is a game we invented for couples to communicate about their primary goals. Imagine that you suddenly have an extra $50,000 or $100,000. What would you do with it as a family? Indulge in some fantasy; don't be limited by what you think is practical.

2. Do you really want to achieve what you decided was the fantasy for the money you've just mythically received? If so, try to fathom that it wouldn't be altogether impossible, if you're willing to make that goal your prime motivation.

3. Now we're going to finish identifying your motivations and goals on your Primary Motivations and Payoffs chart in the appendix. This time we'll look at actual conditions, not just feelings.

3a. *Directed From.* What conditions or circumstances exist in your life that you would like to correct or eliminate? What material objects or life situations exist or persist in your daily life that you want to get rid of (e.g., a car that continually needs repair, a job that's not satisfying, an undesirable residential situation, debt)? Fill in your chart now.

3b. *Directed Toward.* Imagine yourself sitting here today having achieved those things you really want. Specifically, what would be on the list (e.g., a new car, a fulfilling career, a vacation home)? Fill in your chart now. Keep it real. Don't use blue-sky thinking here. If it's not something you're willing to take action on, it doesn't belong on this list.

4. Compare your chart to your spouse's. Where do they overlap? Where are they different?

5. How many of your spouse's values were you aware of? Does this surprise you?

6. What's influencing how you spend?

7. How authentic are your motivations relative to their origin? Are your motivations a result of peer or public pressure, or a result of your own wants? Too often we hear goals that people seem to think they should want or cite.

5

Gaining Control:
A Cash Flow Plan

any people manage money by default: they tend to put off planning their finances until it's too late for planning and they have to react. They take home their paychecks, pay their bills, and then spend the rest as long as it lasts, augmenting their cash with credit. Many other couples make a good faith effort at managing their money, but are frustrated when they realize they are still only reacting to external forces.

Despite the old adage that the only real certainties in life are death and taxes, we all make decisions based on the necessities of survival. Financially, this "default" means paying rent or making a mortgage payment; paying certain bills, such as utilities, car payments, telephone, credit card minimums; going to work; and, of course, paying taxes. Most people walk through life in the shadow of "this is what I have to do." This perception of helplessness dominates their activities and their attitude about money, and they administer their earnings based on default.

Much of how we deal with money has to do with what we

are afraid will happen if we fail to meet these perceived obligations. You pay the bills for fear that a collection agency will knock on your door. The consequences don't seem worth the satisfaction of saying no: the landlord will evict you; the mortgage company will foreclose; the phone company will cut off your service; and the electric company will leave you in the dark. Most people tend to operate as if dominated by an unseen authority, a social parent in the form of an unbending creditor who can be insistent and sometimes downright nasty.

When you live by design, on the other hand, rather than by default, you determine your choices according to your goals and desires. It is active rather than reactive: you take the initiative. In the end, your obligations may be the same, but the difference is that you have chosen to fulfill them. Things you previously felt pressured to do—like buy a birthday present for your mother-in-law or save money to buy a much-needed washing machine—can become less distressing once you take an active role in planning them.

Default and design involve questions of preference. People generally don't *prefer* to pay their phone bills, but they *do* prefer to give gifts—often to the detriment of their cash flow. Many of us tend to give beyond our means, but we never seem to pay bills beyond our means. No one ever says, "I'm a little short of cash this month, but I think I'll send the phone company a big fat check." But many of our cash-strapped clients have rationalized: "Well, I can't really afford to buy my best friend this watch she's been wanting, but I'll stretch a little because I really want to give it to her."

The most balanced and complete design incorporates expenditures that you want to make, those you need to make, and those you've been making anyway. Again, consider what you really want. If you have to work for something, what would make it pay off? Is it a certain car? A knock-out suit? A trip? A musical instrument? What's really going to matter to you? This is where we start designing your cash flow plan. Your attitude will shift to "How can I make this happen?" Once you start believing in what you can accomplish, you will live by design instead of by default.

Richard and Andrea Moore were a class example of default spenders. They both grew up in homes in which money was a little tight. Andrea's mother managed the finances in her family, while her father drank up much of their so-called disposable income. Andrea remembers her mother paying the bills each month, sitting at the kitchen table after dinner with the bills spread out in front of her, her checkbook to her left, her composition book to her right. Andrea knew better than to even walk into the kitchen while her mother was paying the bills and planning the family budget. Andrea started earning her own money when she was twelve years old by babysitting and always saved some of her money in a savings account because her mother said she should.

Richard's parents were default spenders, and not wealthy. Usually the last week of every month was meager. The family ate a lot of cheese sandwiches, oatmeal, and vegetable casseroles. From the time he was ten, Richard had always earned his own money, but no one had ever taught him how to manage it. His adult spending habits were much like his parents'—spend until it's gone and then somehow get by.

Early in their marriage, Richard and Andrea agreed that they should have a budget. As teachers, they had to deal with reduced cash flow during the summer. Andrea's perspective was that all families had budgets and so should she and Richard. Richard felt they needed a budget or they risked falling prey to the miserable habits he had learned from his family's mismanagement.

Unfortunately, neither of them knew anything about personal financial planning. So when Andrea and Richard sat down to plan their family finances every month, it was like trying to collect water in a sieve. They felt they managed their money very tightly, but in reality they never had a firm grip on either predicting or evaluating their expenditures. When they listed their outgoing cash, they never included entertainment or vacations. "Entertainment and vacations are what you do if there's any money left over," Richard reasoned. "You shouldn't put them in the budget."

In practice, however, the Moores ate out a couple of times a week because they were too busy to cook or felt the need to get out of the house. And they took at least one airplane trip to visit relatives every year. Because these expenses were not in the plan, they used credit cards.

This is default spending, which creates a domino effect. The trips and meals out charged to credit become part of the "have-to" payments the Moores must include in their budget. Because every time they use their credit cards their minimum monthly obligation rises, there is even less "left over" for entertainment and trips. The budget becomes even tighter, and doing the other things they want to do becomes increasingly impossible. So, to finance their eating out and vacations, they turn to credit cards again.

Default spending and default budgeting don't take into account a couple's spending behavior, emotions, or other external forces, like peer pressure. Another factor in default budgeting is deception. When asked what they spend on entertainment each month, one couple replied thoughtfully, "Well, last weekend alone we spent $160. So, figure about $400 a month." They must have a very clever calculator that multiplies $160 by four and gets $400. When they do budget, people tend to budget what they think they *should* spend, rather than what they really spend.

Default spending also arises from a common, if often subconscious, attitude that credit cards are not the same as real money. Another relatively affluent couple revealed that they spend $25 a week eating out. Twenty-five dollars could hardly buy sandwiches at a deli for one person in a work week. What this couple were really saying was that they spend $25 a week *in cash* eating out. The rest is on credit cards, which they don't perceive as real money because it's a deferred transaction.

Designed Spending: The Family Cash Flow Plan

Instead of default, look at design. Not too many years ago, a unique form of designed financing—the layaway plan—was the most common form of buying major purchases when cash was not at hand. Our parents probably used the layaway plan to buy new living room furniture, a television, or other home-oriented necessities. Many of us have used a layaway plan to buy our first bicycle. The trick with the layaway plan was that you purchased an item and paid it off over time without interest, but you took the item home *after* it was paid for. Today's charge-and-carry world is just the opposite.

Layaway has had its day as a force in consumer spending, so we will have to manage our money better on our own. The family cash flow plan we have developed, which has been effective for thousands of our clients, will help you end the special financial problems of the two-income family, turn the family bottom line from red to black, and liberate money to meet the family goals. Specifically, the plan

- Fosters an understanding between you and your spouse regarding your attitude and financial preferences
- Provides an emotionally and psychologically satisfactory approach to determining the specific financial duties of each spouse
- Tracks how much money you bring in and where it goes
- Furnishes realistic methods for coping with the extra costs of a two-income family
- Demonstrates how you can use liberated money to wipe your family financial slate clear of debt
- Helps you achieve your goals for personal savings and investment

The first aspect of the plan to keep in mind is the Primary Motivations and Payoffs chart from the appendix that you worked on following chapters 3 and 4. This chart combines your and your spouse's goals and is key because it identifies and clarifies those values and goals that are most significant to your satisfaction with money.

We asked you to address your motivations and payoffs in two areas: the feeling or emotion that you experience regarding financial issues and life aspirations; and the actual achievement or condition you desire, such as buying a house or getting out of debt.

As you begin to design your family's spending plan, you will use these motivations and payoffs to determine your destination. One of the advantages of the Primary Motivations and Payoffs chart is that it is a reference tool for later use, particularly when you and your spouse become confused or frustrated about where you are going. Setting up a cash flow plan will not suddenly make a fairy tale out of your finances. You will no doubt encounter some bumps in the road, as the Weatherses did.

Kirby and Denise Weathers had been following the plan for three months when Denise called, nearly in tears, because their plan seemed to be falling apart. She confessed that she had believed, despite our advice to the contrary, that setting up the plan would solve their family's problems instantly. Sitting down at the dining room table and identifying common goals was easy enough. "It was almost romantic," Denise said wistfully. "We really knew what we wanted. But then unexpected circumstances started getting in the way. Once, some friends came in from out of town and we took them to a show. It wasn't in our spending plan. We used our credit cards to pay for $120 worth of theater tickets. Another time, we were just at the end of our ropes. The kids were making us crazy, so we went to the country for the weekend. That was another $400 on credit." Added Kirby, "It was easy to see that following the money spending plan was a good idea, but it was sometimes hard to do it once we left the table."

The Weatherses' experience is common. We all know that it's easier to make resolutions than to stick to them. Kirby and Denise needed to be reassured that their goals were important and worthwhile, and we encouraged them to put themselves and their goals first. The next time friends showed up, Kirby and Denise let the guests split the bill with them; they spent within their preset entertainment budget. When they wanted a weekend alone, they asked another couple to take the children and enjoyed a romantic escape at home. A few months later, they reciprocated.

Another pitfall for many people is postponing reality until they've "had enough fun." They succumb to their secondary goals before they even consider their primary one. Andy and Ellen Wilson were a classic case: "Well, now that I've bought my new sports car, I can come see you and work on a plan," Andy said. They had plunged further into debt, acquired something they "really" wanted, and then were "ready" to move ahead with the plan. After they'd finally begun working toward their real goals and aspirations, they regarded the sports car as an albatross and sold it. "I still can't believe I bought the car," Ellen said. "I was behaving like an impetuous little girl."

The experiences of the Wilsons and the Weatherses are not uncommon. Temptation will come, and inevitably you will spend money you hadn't expected to spend. That's why evaluating your primary motivations and payoffs regularly is so important. It will regalvanize your determination and validate your goals. You will be able to point back to it and say: "This is what we really want. Let's work for this." It's a way to regroup, reaffirm your commitment, and move ahead.

After the Primary Motivations and Payoffs information comes the body of the plan, which involves three main components: income, expenses, and backup data. And, like the Primary Motivations and Payoffs, each has a distinct function and purpose in the overall plan. We will discuss each component in this and the following chapters. Blank forms for recording and assessing your financial condition are provided in the appendix. Use these forms as models from which to assemble your own data and plan.

Determining Your Income

Writing down how much money you make may seem like a kindergarten task, but a surprising number of people don't know their annual income. Many people spend as though their gross income is their actual take-home pay. Many others don't realize what they pay in taxes. One couple told us, "We didn't pay any taxes last year; we got a refund." They had lost sight of the fact that taxes had already been deducted from their paychecks every week.

Under "Income" in your cash flow plan, you will determine your projected gross and net (spendable) income from all sources; your actual monthly income; and the actual deductions from your income. By identifying each of your incomes by source, you will have a much clearer picture of how much you earn and what happens to it even before you start to spend it.

Troy and Christine Taylor had a vague idea of their combined income, but they couldn't be sure. An accountant calculated their taxes, and they merely glanced at the results before signing and filing the forms. When they sat down to fill out the Projected Income form, they stared at it as if it were written in hieroglyphics.

"I don't really know how much I make," Troy said. "I think my gross is about $55,000. Christine makes about $40,000, but she also does some work on the side, and so do I. We figure we're going to break $100,000 this year, but I don't know how much of it is really ours after the government gets its pound of flesh." Many people routinely excuse their ignorance of their own financial lives by passing the buck: "I don't really look at my check"; or "I give my check to my wife and she handles it"; or "It's deposited automatically by my company and I often don't pick up my pay stub to find out what went where."

By carefully reviewing their pay stubs, Troy and Christine were able to see their actual gross and net income. By checking their bank deposits, they determined their projected income for additional work during the year and savings account interest. Troy's instinct was correct—they broke the $100,000 mark. As you can see in the chart on page 59, there was quite a difference between their gross and net income figures. From this discovery point, Troy and Christine wanted to find a way to track what they really earned on a monthly basis—no more guesswork.

The Actual Monthly Income statement served that purpose, showing the Taylors' actual net cash per month. This statement also provides a means of observing how income rises (or, we

Income	Monthly		Annual	
	Net	*Gross*	*Net*	*Gross*
Client #1 Salary Troy	3000	4583	36,000	55,000
Client #2 Salary Christine	2150	3333	25,800	40,000
Client #1 Free-lance Earnings Troy	167	167	2000	2000
Client #2 Free-lance Earnings Christine	417	417	5000	5000
Commissions				
Bonuses				
Child Support				
Interest	58	58	700	700
Dividends				
Loan Proceeds				
Rental Property				
Other _____				
_____				
Total	5792	8558	69,500	102,700

ACTUAL MONTHLY INCOME

Year:	Jan	Feb	Mar	Apr	May
Client #1 Salary (net) Troy	3000	3000	3000	3000	3000
Client #2 Salary (net) Christine	2150	2150	2150	2200	2200
Client #1 Free-lance Earnings Troy	0	500	0	0	300
Client #2 Free-lance Earnings Christine	0	450	200	200	500
Commissions					
Bonuses					
Child Support					
Interest	50	54	58	60	65
Dividends					
Loan Proceeds					
Rental Property					
Tax Refund					
Other Sources of Income					
Total Monthly Income	5200	6154	5408	5460	6065

Jun	Jul	Aug	Sep	Oct	Nov	Dec	Total
3000							
2200							
0							
300							
70							
5570							

ACTUAL DEDUCTIONS FROM INCOME

Year of Deduction:		Jan	Feb	Mar	Apr	May
Federal Income Tax (FIT)	T	754	754	754	754	754
	C	624	624	624	644	644
State Income Tax (SIT)	T	234	234	234	234	234
	C	186	186	186	190	190
Social Security (FICA)	T	350	350	350	350	350
	C	255	255	255	260	260
State Disability (SDI)	T	5	5	5	5	5
	C	3	3	3	4	4
Life/Disability Insurance						
Health Insurance						
Pension Plan	T	90	90	90	90	90
	C	65	65	65	70	70
Profit Sharing						
Savings	T	50	50	50	50	50
	C	50	50	50	50	50
Stock Option Plan (ESOP)						
Contributions						
Loan Payment	T	100	100	100	100	100
	C	0	0	0	0	0
Union Dues						
Other						
Total	T	1583	1583	1583	1583	1583
	C	1183	1183	1183	1218	1218

Jun	Jul	Aug	Sep	Oct	Nov	Dec	Total
754 644							
234 190							
350 260							
5 4							
90 70							
50 50							
100 0							
1583 1218							

hesitate to add, falls). Once you know how much money you make and how much you can expect to make in the future, you will be able to pursue your goals more realistically.

The next form, Actual Deductions from Income, helped the Taylors pinpoint how much is deducted from their paychecks for federal, state, and local taxes; pension plans; health insurance; union dues; and other set obligations. They found the information easily accessible on their pay stubs; they simply did not want to look before. After completing the form, they saw just how much money was going to taxes; through better planning, they could put it to work earning equity.

Tracking Your Expenses

The ultimate decisions in design versus default are made when you begin to examine your expenses: here you learn where all that money goes. Knowledge and awareness are the first steps toward control and design. By considering each and every expenditure, you can identify what is really important to you—and what is not.

Incredible as it may seem, most people spend from 30 to 100 percent more than they earn. On average, the couples we work with have a negative cash flow (aided by credit cards) of $1,000 a month. That adds up quickly to a significant sum of money. In chapter 6, you will identify and list all monthly expenses from mortgage payments to clothes to car repairs. As a result, you will learn to set boundaries for your discretionary spending and begin to see what percent of your money goes, or should go, to paying off your debt and building savings.

Identifying their expenses helped Jake and Teri Bacon realize how much they were spending on music. They had bought a compact-disc player a year before they came to see us and were still rounding out their music collection, spending about $50 a week on compact discs, trying to replace vinyl records from Abba to ZZ Top. Teri's jaw dropped when she saw the final expense sheet. "I had no idea we were spending so much on music. And you know what? Every time we shopped for music, it was preceded by breakfast out at our favorite place near the music store."

For Jennifer Owens, the expense sheet provided the ammunition she had been looking for. Henry, her husband of five years, had a tendency to buy "too many" books. "He'd read the *New York Times Book Review* on Sunday morning and on Sunday afternoon would head to the bookstore to stock up on recommended titles—hardcover only, of course. He has hardly read any of them. How can you read all the books you buy when you buy three a week? The way I saw it, his book-buying binges were cutting into our desire to trim debt and take some short vacations." As penance, Henry agreed to read the books he has before he buys any more, and to visit the public library more often.

Gathering Supporting Data

The final aspect of the plan brings together related data to give you a broader perspective on your financial condition. You will be asked to record these data at the end of chapter 6. On the Debts and Liabilities form, you will list your short- and long-term debts and liabilities—from credit cards to taxes to any kind of debt requiring regular payments. As the items and amounts on this list shrink from month to month, your incentive to reduce spending will grow stronger. The reward of acquiring a new rowing machine or a VCR will pale next to the satisfaction of watching the debt column fade away. "It actually got to the point that I was excited to see what was happening on the debt list," said Emily Landreth. She and her husband, Todd, wiped out $8,000 of debt in one year. "It helped us spend less each month because we really wanted to see those numbers go down," Todd added.

The next form is the Financial Statement, which identifies your assets and liabilities and helps you determine your net worth (assets minus liabilities).

Finally, we will ask you to complete an Insurance Summary, which addresses all of the insurance programs you have— health, dental, life, auto, property, liability, and so on. Insurance, like total income, is one area that is hazy for most couples. When asked what kind of health insurance they have, most people know only the scantest information. In response to our inquiries about his company's health coverage, Todd Landreth said, "I'm in a group plan." "Well," we asked, "what kind of coverage do you have? What's the out-of-pocket cost to you? What's the deductible?" Todd didn't know, and neither do most.

One of the advantages to this cash flow plan is that you do not need a background in accounting to use it. There are no complicated bookkeeping rules to learn, and you can do it without a computer. Another aspect of the plan is that data are easily retrievable so that taking care of your family finances will take minutes instead of hours.

‖‖‖   CHECKPOINT 5   ‖‖‖

Managing your money by default will only send you tail-spinning into a downward spiral, but if you approach your family spending by design to include all items from dinners out to car insurance, you will regain the control you lost.

1. Are you a default or a design spender? What about your spouse?

2. How would you characterize your spending patterns?

3. How many times have you sat down to draw up a family budget? How successful have your family budgets been?

4. When was the last time you spent money on something that was a surprise, such as out-of-town guests? How did you feel about spending the money? On what else could it have been spent?

5. Fill out the Projected Income form included in the appendix, to give yourself a clearer picture of your own financial condition. Also fill out a sample or representative month on the Actual Monthly Income and Actual Deductions from Income forms. You may have to dig for some of the numbers, but the forms are straightforward, and most of the information can be gleaned from your pay stubs and statements from banks.

6

The Bottom Line

or David and Beverly Miller, following a cash flow plan was key to their family's financial turn-around. By identifying their common goals and setting their course, the Millers were able to liberate an average $845 a month from their spending; now, instead of going $10,000 a year into the hole, they spend and save only what they really have.

The Millers earned $100,000 a year from David's business as an electronics consultant ($75,000) and Beverly's job as a teacher ($25,000). Their two daughters, ages six and eight, attended private schools. And while the Millers appeared to be sitting pretty, they were actually uncomfortable. The couple had been unable to achieve what they really wanted—financial security. They owned their own home and drove cars their neighbors envied, but they suffered increasing anxiety about the family's level of financial stability and flexibility.

"It occurred to me one day when I was laid up with a pulled hamstring from playing basketball with a bunch of 25-year-old engineers," David said drily, "that if I really got hurt or killed, we'd be up a creek. We had no savings, just debt up to our ears.

As macho as it sounds, I'm the primary breadwinner. And since I'm self-employed, if I don't work, I don't make money."

Beverly would lie awake at night going through "worst-case scenarios" when David was away on business. What if he got killed in a plane crash? What if he suffered an incapacitating stroke? "I suffer from my mom's affliction. I'm a big worrywart. I worry about everything. David teases me about it. Even the girls tease me about it. Sometimes David and I fight about it. But I really was growing to hate the feeling of floating along knowing that at any instant we could come crashing down and there wouldn't be a cushion for us to land on."

Beverly exaggerated her own fears, but the family's concerns were real and had to be addressed. By most accounts, the Millers are considered well-off, but they felt anything but affluent. They spent money independently of each other; both were insufficiently aware of what the other was doing or why and blamed each other. Beverly thought David's expensive toys kept the family from saving money; David thought that Beverly spent it all, without regard to how hard he worked for it.

Without a common goal or even an understanding of the other's wishes, the Millers managed to accumulate $10,000 of new debt every year. They refinanced their home three times to pay off debt—after all, the house was appreciating each year. They continually dipped into their greatest asset, which would have given them the financial security they sought, to support their lifestyle and their loose spending behavior. "We make a lot of money," Beverly said unabashedly. "You'd think we wouldn't have these troubles. I actually feel we make enough money, or I'd be working at something else, even though I'm doing what I really love. We ought to be able to have exactly what we want."

What Beverly hadn't taken into consideration was the real cost of their lifestyle. Once you have indulged in luxury, you begin to feel that those indulgences reflect your concrete position in society, rather than the position to which you aspire and can emulate with the credit illusion. The Millers, with their spacious house and comfortable lifestyle, spent freely. Dinners out, movies out, new bedroom sets for the girls—all on credit. Given these unconscious spending patterns, it was tough for the Millers to change their behavior. Change requires awareness of a problem. As the strain became increasingly unbearable, they realized they needed to do something. David's trouble with his hamstring got them talking.

Telling the Truth

It had been quite some time since Beverly and David had discussed their goals. Backed by their resolve to turn the tide of their financial dilemma, they analyzed their motivations and payoffs.

FEELINGS/EMOTIONS

Directed Toward	Directed From
security	uncertainty
prepared for the future	unprepared
comfortable	disconcerted
calm	anxious
grounded	at loose ends

MOTIVATIONS/PAYOFFS

Directed Toward	Directed From
solvency	debt
emergency savings	no financial cushion
retirement savings	no plans for the future

As you can see, the Millers are most concerned with making sure their family is more secure and financially prepared. With two small children, they are both worried that they have nothing in place to care for the family should hard times arise. Because

one of their major goals was to reduce debt, their first step was
to scrutinize their current situation. The Debts and Liabilities
list provided the backup data they needed regarding their various debts—credit cards, loans, and installment payments. For
each liability, they now knew the exact balance due, the annual
interest rate, the monthly payment (the minimum, in some cases), and due date. They couldn't believe how quickly the amount
of debt had grown, but it felt good to be addressing it.

Now came the part that would give the Millers the information they needed to begin achieving their goals—the Expense
Guide. The Expense Guide provided in the plan helps to estimate monthly fixed and variable operating expenses, household
expenses, and debt payments (as listed on Debts and Liabilities). Because the Millers, like many couples, were not in the
habit of tracking or watching their spending, they used their
checkbook register and recent bills to determine amounts for
their Expense Guide. In some cases, household expenses, for
example, they estimated figures for which they did not have
exact amounts. They knew they would be keeping a close eye on
their spending from now on, so their estimates could always be
adjusted if they turned out to be inaccurate. Right now, the task
was to reduce their overspending and find a way of allocating
dollars toward their goals.

In the Expense portion of the plan, the Millers identified four
distinct savings needs related to nonmonthly expenses, emergency funds, and investment needs. The Millers opted to open
four separate accounts so that they could see more clearly how
much money was set aside for certain expenses and so they
would not be tempted to "borrow" money earmarked for insurance to pay for Christmas gifts. The four accounts serve the
following needs:

- One to Four Payments a Year—amounts and due dates
  are known
- Periodic/Nonmonthly—amounts and due dates vary
- Reserve—a target amount is preset
- Investment and Major Purchases

DEBTS AND LIABILITIES

	TOTAL BALANCE	INTEREST RATE	MONTHLY PAYMENT	DATE DUE

I. CREDIT CARDS

	TOTAL BALANCE	INTEREST RATE	MONTHLY PAYMENT	DATE DUE
1. Sears	1200	18%	50	20th
2. Macy's	250	19%	25	20th
3. Citibank Pref. Visa	2400	19%	100	5th
4. First Federal Visa	1800	19%	75	10th
5. Hanover Mastercard	900	19%	50	12th
6.				
7.				
8.				
Subtotal	6550		300	

II. LOANS

	TOTAL BALANCE	INTEREST RATE	MONTHLY PAYMENT	DATE DUE
1. America S & L	120,000	9%	1215	1st
2. Equity Line	35,000	12%	320	1st
3. Auto Loan	15,000	13½%	440	15th
4.				
5.				
Subtotal	170,000		1975	

	TOTAL BALANCE	INTEREST RATE	MONTHLY PAYMENT	DATE DUE

III. TAXES

1. Federal—year _____				
2. State—year _____				
3. Property—year _____				
4. Other _____				
Subtotal				

IV. MISCELLANEOUS

1.				
2.				
3.				
4.				
5.				
6.				
Subtotal				

Grand Total				

The One to Four Payments a Year Account is for known expenses that arise at specific times during the year in predetermined amounts. Following is the section of the Expense Guide outlining the Millers' annual needs. By determining what their total needs would be, the Millers were able to identify by simple division how much money they needed to deposit into this account each month. These monthly deposits meant that when the item was due to be paid, the necessary funds were already set aside, ensuring prompt and easy payment.

One to Four Payments a Year Account

Auto Registration	$25
Dues/Licenses/Publications	25
Insurance	
Auto	monthly
Health/Dental	monthly
Disability	none
Life	100
Home	70
Property/Rental	0
Other	0
Taxes	
Federal	1,000
State	380
Property	200
Other	0
Tax Preparation/Professional Fees	35
Subtotal/Amount Saved per Month	$1,835

The Periodic/Nonmonthly Account covers expenses that arise on an annual basis. These expenses do not have specific due dates and amounts, nor are they obligatory, although most people consider them necessary. The Millers estimated these amounts and then agreed to operate within their estimates to help choose and control spending. As the funds in this account accumulated, the couple was able to base their purchasing choices and timing upon the actual cash balance in the family account. This approach helped answer such questions as: Can we afford to buy this? Can we do it now? What will we be trading off, if anything? Is it worth the tradeoffs to do it now?

In this way, the Millers found out what they had to save each month in order to afford such things as clothing, holiday and miscellaneous gifts, travel, minor home furnishings, and charitable contributions. This is the account that shrunk as the Millers determined that they were spending on things they easily could trim, such as vacation travel. The total per month to save came to $1805.

Periodic/Nonmonthly Account

Clothing	$650
Gifts	300
Travel/Vacation	420
Furniture/Appliances	50
Contributions	50
Continuing Education	0
Home Maintenance/Repair	100
Auto Maintenance/Repair	100
Health Maintenance	135
Subtotal/Amount Saved per Month	$1,805

The target amount for the Reserve Account is determined differently because this fund serves occasions that usually come up with little or no notice. The Millers had to decide how much they needed to set aside in actual liquidity to carry them through periods of lost income due to disability, or reductions in David's income. If David lost his ability to work, the family could not have survived on Beverly's $25,000 income. If Beverly lost her ability to work, however, the family would be less inconvenienced. The Millers determined that three months was the longest David would probably be laid up should anything happen to him. They decided to set aside $25,000 to use in the event either one of them lost a job or the capacity to work.

The Reserve Account is also the holding bin for such items as insurance deductibles, repair and replacement costs, and out-of-pocket medical and dental bills. With a total of $32,400 in needs and $10,000 already set aside, the Millers were able to begin with almost a third of their goal and accumulate the remainder over time. They determined the amount needed for this account by reviewing their insurance policies, evaluating the condition of the house and cars, and recalling how much emergencies had cost them the year before.

Reserve Account

Loss of Income	$24,000
Insurance Deduction	1,400
Repair/Replacement	5,000
Emergency Medical/Dental	2,000
Total Amount Needed	$32,400
Starting Balance	10,000
Amount to Save per Month	0

The fourth account, the Investment and Major Purchases Account, represents such items as an individual retirement account, children's college education, a major vacation, or major purchases. Unlike the others, this account has a long-term outlook rather than an annual outlook. When they set out to take charge of their financial situation, the Millers said they were most concerned about their family's security, of which one aspect was addressed in the Reserve Account. The Millers did not plan to make any major purchases from this account, choosing to concentrate only on the investments. In order to put away $4,000 in retirement funds and $5,000 for college tuition, the Millers discovered they would have to save $750 a month in the Investment and Major Purchases Account. The monthly or periodic contributions to the account are initially made from the money "saved" by cutting other expenses or generated from increases in personal earnings, income tax refunds, bonuses, or inheritances.

Investment and Major Purchases Account

IRA/Keogh	$4,000
Children's Education	5,000
Real Estate Purchase	0
Major Vacation	0
Total Amount Needed	**$9,000**
Starting Balance	0
Amount to Save per Month	**$750**

In addition to the information gathered regarding income and expenses, an overall Financial Statement and an Insurance Summary is useful. It's a good idea to record the data before you plan your strategy for correcting your negative cash flow. By providing accurate asset and liability information, the Financial Statement will enable you to determine what resources and options you have available for sale or as collateral for loans. The Insurance Summary provides a comprehensive assessment of your coverages and specifies the premium and possible cost to you if an insurance claim is made. You will be asked to complete these forms at the end of this chapter.

The Millers were now ready to begin addressing their negative cash flow. As illustrated in the following Expense Guide, once their expenses were totaled, the Millers discovered they were spending $845 more a month than they brought in.

Since David and Beverly already felt they were squeezing as much as possible out of their income, they had to approach solutions from a different angle. They enjoyed their lifestyle and had no desire to lose it; however, with their identified mutual goals fresh on their minds, they started to evaluate each purchase in light of goals that were more important.

A few items could be jettisoned without causing either David or Beverly to wince. They both agreed to keep a watchful eye on such discretionary expenses as clothing, gifts, and travel. In fact, they were embarrassed to have "gotten away with" uncontrolled spending on those things anyway. Now they had a reason and a plan to follow. In three categories, they discovered they

EXPENSE GUIDE

Name MILLER	Date JAN. 1st

	PRO-JECTED EXPENSE	MO. 1 ACTUAL	MO. 2 ACTUAL	MO. 3 ACTUAL	YEAR-TO-DATE TOTALS

OPERATING EXPENSES—FIXED

	PRO-JECTED EXPENSE	MO. 1 ACTUAL	MO. 2 ACTUAL	MO. 3 ACTUAL	YEAR-TO-DATE TOTALS
AUTO LEASE					
CABLE TV		20			
CHILD CARE		200			
CHILDREN'S PROGRAMS		25			
INSURANCE					
AUTO		150			
DISABILITY		0			
HEALTH		300			
LIFE		100			
RENT		0			
SCHOOL TUITION		500			
SUBTOTALS—FIXED		1295			

	PRO-JECTED EXPENSE	MO. 1 ACTUAL	MO. 2 ACTUAL	MO. 3 ACTUAL	YEAR-TO-DATE TOTALS

OPERATING EXPENSES—VARIABLE

	PRO-JECTED EXPENSE	MO. 1 ACTUAL	MO. 2 ACTUAL	MO. 3 ACTUAL	YEAR-TO-DATE TOTALS
CHILDREN'S MISC. NEEDS		25			
CLUB DUES/EXTRAS		0			
GARBAGE		20			
GAS/ELECTRIC		160			
HOUSEKEEPER/GARDENER		80			
POOL/SPA SERVICE		0			
TELEPHONE		150			
WATER		20			
SUBTOTALS—VARIABLE		455			

EXPENSE GUIDE

	PRO-JECTED EXPENSE	MO. 1 ACTUAL	MO. 2 ACTUAL	MO. 3 ACTUAL	YEAR-TO-DATE TOTALS

HOUSEHOLD EXPENSES

	PRO-JECTED EXPENSE	MO. 1 ACTUAL	MO. 2 ACTUAL	MO. 3 ACTUAL	YEAR-TO-DATE TOTALS
FOOD/MISC. HOUSEHOLD ITEMS		400			
FOOD OUT/RESTAURANTS		400			
ENTERTAINMENT		100			
LAUNDRY/DRY CLEANING		80			
GAS/PARKING/TOLLS/ TICKETS		200			
PUBLIC TRANSPORTATION		0			
BABYSITTING		40			
PET CARE		0			
SELF-CARE (e.g., Manicure, Facial)		50			
COUNSELING/THERAPY		0			
MINOR MEDICAL		25			
MISC. OTHER (e.g., Postage, Books, CDs)		30			
SUBTOTALS—HOUSEHOLD		1325			

	PRO-JECTED EXPENSE	MO. 1 ACTUAL	MO. 2 ACTUAL	MO. 3 ACTUAL	YEAR-TO-DATE TOTALS

DEBT PAYMENTS

	PRO-JECTED EXPENSE	MO. 1 ACTUAL	MO. 2 ACTUAL	MO. 3 ACTUAL	YEAR-TO-DATE TOTALS
MORTGAGE #1		1215			
MORTGAGE #2					
EQUITY LINE		320			
INSTALLMENT LOANS					
AUTO #1		440			
AUTO #2					
COMPUTER/FURNITURE		180			
BANK/CREDIT UNION					
PRIVATE/FAMILY #1					
PRIVATE/FAMILY #2					
STUDENT LOANS					
CREDIT CARD PAYMENTS					
DEPT. STORE #1		50			
DEPT. STORE #2		25			
DEPT. STORE #3					
VISA/MASTERCARD #1		100			
VISA/MASTERCARD #2		75			
VISA/MASTERCARD #3		50			
GAS CARD #1					
GAS CARD #2					
TAXES					
FEDERAL					
STATE					
DOCTORS/DENTISTS					
SUBTOTALS—DEBT		2455			

EXPENSE GUIDE

	PRO-JECTED EXPENSE	MO. 1 ACTUAL	MO. 2 ACTUAL	MO. 3 ACTUAL	YEAR-TO-DATE TOTALS

ONE TO FOUR PAYMENTS A YEAR EXPENSES

	PRO-JECTED EXPENSE	MO. 1 ACTUAL	MO. 2 ACTUAL	MO. 3 ACTUAL	YEAR-TO-DATE TOTALS
AUTO REGISTRATION	25				
DUES/LICENSES/PUBLICATIONS	25				
INSURANCE					
AUTO	MONTHLY				
HEALTH/DENTAL	MONTHLY				
DISABILITY	0				
LIFE	100				
HOME	70				
PROPERTY/RENTAL	0				
TAXES					
FEDERAL	1000				
STATE	380				
PROPERTY	200				
TAX PREPARATION/PROFESSIONAL FEES	35				
SUBTOTALS/AMOUNT SAVED PER MONTH	1835				

PERIODIC/NONMONTHLY EXPENSES

CLOTHING	650				
GIFTS	300				
TRAVEL/VACATION	420				
FURNITURE/APPLIANCES	50				
CONTRIBUTIONS	50				
CONTINUING EDUCATION	0				
HOME MAINTENANCE/REPAIR	100				
AUTO MAINTENANCE/REPAIR	100				
HEALTH MAINTENANCE	135				
SUBTOTALS/AMOUNT SAVED PER MONTH	1805				

	PRO-JECTED EXPENSE	MO. 1 ACTUAL	MO. 2 ACTUAL	MO. 3 ACTUAL	YEAR-TO-DATE TOTALS

SAVINGS

RESERVE					
INVESTMENT AND MAJOR PURCHASES					

GRAND TOTAL EXPENSES		$ 9170	$	$	$

<8333> INCOME

DEPOSITS TO SAVINGS

ONE TO FOUR PAYMENTS A YEAR EXPENSES					
PERIODIC/NONMONTHLY EXPENSES					
RESERVE					
INVESTMENT AND MAJOR PURCHASES					

could reduce their spending by $535 a month. "It was exciting to think the holidays could come and go without leaving behind mountains of credit card bills. We were always paying off Christmas well into April. That was ridiculous," Beverly said. David, an admitted clotheshorse, added, "I know I have enough clothes to keep me happy for a long time. I like ties and I like rugby shirts. But you should see my closet. I could probably keep Wall Street and a New Zealand rugby team outfitted for a decade."

They also made a decision about family vacations—to plan them carefully. Instead of waiting until the last minute and then forking over a few thousand dollars for a family trip to Hawaii, the Millers realized they could save money and have more fun by planning far enough ahead. In addition to lower advance airfares, they could redeem some of the miles on frequent-flier programs. "I fly around so much I make Air Force One look like part of the Moth Ball Fleet," David said. "But I never joined a frequent-flier program. I was always rushing to catch flights, and I never thought they were worth anything." Added Beverly, "We also started looking at vacations closer to home. Instead of hopping on a plane to get the heck out of Portland, we started driving around the Pacific Northwest. My family took car trips when I was little and I didn't want my little girls to grow up thinking you had to take a plane to go on vacation." Since they started planning their vacations and involving the girls in the planning, they have had more fun.

Other areas demanding change required more thought and consideration, and a little humble pie. The private school to which the Millers proudly sent their daughters was a bone of contention. Frankly, Beverly thought the highly rated public school in the neighborhood was fine, but David felt that a "man in his position" should send his kids to a private school. Beverly yielded. The private school *would* help get the girls into a good college prep school and then into a good college. As the two girls got older and as David's career became more visible and he began to work with some private investment firms, he felt he needed the social boost that private schools provided. Both

David and Beverly acknowledged that the public schools in their neighborhood were among the best in the area, but David was still reluctant. "It's like calling them up to the majors and then sending them down after the first game," David said. "Most of the kids in our neighborhood go to private schools—and their parents are the big shots that hire consultants like me. You just don't realize how important it is to put forth that image of affluence." Then David sat back in his chair. "Did I just say 'image of affluence'? " he asked with a sheepish grin. "Yup," came the resounding chorus. "Okay, okay. Well, hey, I went to a public school and I guess I turned out all right."

By agreeing to send their daughters to public school (which the girls ultimately preferred because the playground equipment was better), the Millers were able to save $6,000 a year. By the end of the year, David proclaimed public education the best thing since sliced bread. "It's good for the kids to be in school with children who aren't all necessarily as well-off as they are," he said. Beverly rolled her eyes.

Emotion came into the picture when they discussed letting the housekeeper go. They had hired Beatriz as their housekeeper shortly after she had fled from El Salvador. Her husband was working back-to-back jobs, and Beatriz was contributing whatever she could to the family income by cleaning houses. She was also the mother of one of Beverly's former students. The Millers were Beatriz's first employers. When other friends commented about how clean their house was, they mentioned Beatriz, and she soon had a full schedule.

So letting go of Beatriz was a hard decision. At one point in their discussion, Beverly said, "It's only eighty bucks a month. That's not very much." But David reminded her, gently, "Everything's just 'only this much' a month. But it adds up." Finally, the Millers agreed that, in fact, they didn't really *need* a housekeeper. Before they hired Beatriz, David and Beverly shared household chores. Then the girls came along and so much time was devoted to them that the chores suffered. But now the girls were older, old enough to do some chores themselves and, in fact, Beatriz only came twice a month. Telling

Beatriz wasn't going to be easy, but the Millers took comfort in the fact that because they had given her so many referrals, Beatriz could fill the empty time slot almost immediately.

"You know," David commented at the end of one meeting, "we're not just planning our family finances, we're reevaluating our standards and values. We're even teaching our girls the value of work and of being with lots of different kinds of people."

The next item for the Millers' consideration was entertainment. As we have said, many couples, when asked how much they spend on entertainment and restaurant meals, give us answers based on what they think they *should* spend, like Richard and Andrea Moore and their clever calculator. The Millers were no different. It was so easy for them to go out, put the day behind them, relax, and enjoy a casual meal—thanks to their credit cards. They almost never used cash. Why? "I feel guilty when I use cash. Like it should be used for something more important. Groceries, maybe. Paying bills," David said. Consequently, the Millers didn't perceive they were spending much on entertainment—because they never saw real dollars go out of their pockets into the till. They discounted what they purchased on credit cards.

Once we suggested that the Millers start paying for everything in cash, they realized just how much they were spending—and how they couldn't really afford those $150 meals for two. They voluntarily slashed their entertainment spending by an astounding $300 a month, more than half of what they had been spending. This "pay in cash" tactic dramatically reveals the extent of unconscious spending most couples practice. As your awareness is heightened, you can begin to change your behavior.

For their next trick, the Millers confronted irony head-on. A year earlier, David had insisted the family buy a computer to help them budget and track their expenses. He bought a fancy new computer and software that could have balanced the federal budget. "The way I figured it, the computer would motivate us to do something about our financial situation," David said. "But all we did was boot up the software and talk about getting started." Beverly rolled her eyes again. "He wanted me to read the manual and get going," she said. "I hate reading computer manuals. I *won't* read computer manuals." As much as he wanted to believe that he would get the family budget into the computer and start managing it effectively, David finally admitted that he was probably too busy to ever do it. Beverly wasn't going to do it either. Finally, he decided to sell the computer. He already had one for work, anyway. The proceeds from the sale of the computer and the liberated dollars from the monthly payments would go toward the girls' college education fund. Computers can often facilitate the job of managing cash flow, but they are not a magic solution. It still takes some time and communication to work with them.

Within seven months, the Millers had completely reversed their money flow so that they were actually *earning* approximately $1,000 a month more than they were spending and were able to allocate the dollars to new uses. Before they analyzed their extra costs, the Millers were *spending* $845 more than they made a month. The following charts illustrate the Miller family's time line for their financial about-face.

Under their new family cash-flow plan, the Millers discov-

The Millers:
Cutting the Extra Costs

Expense	Initial Budget	Liberated Dollars
Clothing	$ 650	$ 200
Gifts	350	125
Travel	420	210
Private School	500	500
Housekeeper	80	80
Entertainment/Meals Out	500	300
Computer Payment	180	180
	$2,680	$1,595

ered they would have to save $3,855 out of their $8,333 monthly gross income. This represents 46 percent of their combined incomes. It's easy to see how people can continually finance themselves by using debt; however, it's vital to realize the wisdom of basing purchases upon actual accumulated cash. Using cash also helps prevent overspending. Having corralled their other expenditures, the Millers could set themselves on a course to deposit the correct amounts into their savings accounts and watch their financial condition grow more solid each month.

At the end of the data gathering, Beverly Miller, who had been afraid to find out the truth about her family's financial condition, said: "Yes, it was frightening to see all this out in front of us—especially when we realized how poorly prepared we were and how much we spent—from shoes for the girls, to trips to see the grandparents, and lots of dinners in between. But it was well worth the short-term discomfort to reach this point."

In addition to compiling useful and accurate financial information to help them implement their plan, the Millers also achieved a level of self-awareness from which they could take action. Finally, they were out of the dark. In the light of day, they could chart a course and arrive at their destination: secu-

Miller Time Line
for Correction

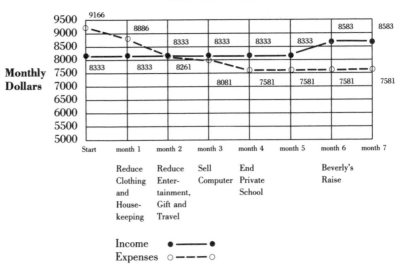

rity. "I feel much safer," David said. "And I don't wince every month when the bills come due. I'm aware of where we stand and have the motivation to spend and save wisely each month. I don't feel that gnawing in my stomach every month any more." Beverly added, "And we don't bicker about money. We can't. It's all right in front of us in black and white. If we disagree about where money is going, we refer back to the plan and generally reach a simple conclusion."

We realize organizing your finances may seem a monumental task. Nevertheless, if you proceed step by step, demonstrating patience and persistence, you will succeed in assembling and implementing your own family cash flow plan.

|||| **CHECKPOINT 6** ||||

Through your steadfast efforts, you can successfully assemble your family cash flow plan, using it to develop a strategy to correct your negative cash flow and embark on the road to financial security.

Turn to the appendix and use the forms provided to complete your Expense Guide, Debts and Liabilities list, Insurance Summary, and Financial Statement.

7

Creating a Family Cash Flow Plan

You have embarked on an exciting journey toward financial health. Now that you and your spouse have discussed your primary motivations and pay-offs and have laid a foundation by gathering your financial data and filling out the forms discussed at the end of chapter 6, you should know how much money you have, where it all goes, and what you have to show for it in the way of acquisitions, savings accounts, or lack thereof. Now, pick up your forms and statements—all of them. We are about to assess your qualitative and quantitative condition. You determined your motivations and payoffs before you found out the truth about your financial situation. Now, with those numbers in hand, you need to examine your desires again.

What did you find out about your financial situation? How did those numbers make you feel? Relieved? Angry? Hopeful? Frustrated? On the brink of taking control? These are the forces you will channel into forming your family cash flow plan.

Let's summarize what you have already learned:

- It's not entirely your fault that you're so deeply in debt, given the evolution of credit cards and the creation of a debt-based society.
- Two-income families can be advantageous, but finances can get out of control because you may be too busy to pay close attention to money matters.
- Emotions can be a powerful force in your family's financial situation.
- Getting waylaid en route to your goals by temptation for more immediate gratification is a common experience.
- Managing money by default is a destructive habit, but managing money by design will help you achieve your family's goals.

It looks clear on paper, doesn't it? But you may be saying, "I've tried budgeting before, it doesn't work. That's why I'm reading this book." What we're talking about isn't just budgeting or setting arbitrary limits on spending. What we propose is that you combine the qualitative with the quantitative. In other words, let emotions and money work together for your happiness, rather than for your discontent.

The family cash flow plan is like a computer language you will use to create your own solution. Applying our suggestions to your own situation will be relatively simple. After all, you're not an accountant working on someone else's expense journal; you are learning to modify your behavior to accomplish your goals. Your habits and emotions have largely created your financial condition, and it's habits and emotions—not just hard numbers—that must be addressed. Anyone can tell you to stop eating out "so much," buying the kids expensive clothes, spending extravagantly on gifts, or picking up a couple of compact discs on a Saturday-afternoon shopping excursion. But that won't help you. That's like going on a liquid diet to shed twenty pounds and then putting thirty pounds back on when you start eating regularly again. You haven't changed your behavior at all. The same goes with your family finances. You and your spouse must be honest about your desires, the forces behind your spending habits, and where you can realistically adjust your spending choices.

Adam and Janis Limacher were fired up about the plan when they began addressing their family's financial crisis. They set their goals, filled out all the forms, and figured out their exact income and expenses. But after six months on the plan, they worried about their lack of progress. Every month, the Expense Guide they filled out revealed that they weren't making any headway against the tide of debt. Although they'd followed the plan faithfully, credit cards kept tripping them up. Adam in particular had a habit of using his credit cards. He had six of them, and when he was feeling a little down, or if he had cause to celebrate, he would buy something—either for himself or for Janis. Finally, Adam had to admit that credit cards were just like cash to him. If he had them, he used them. Reluctantly, Adam put all of his credit cards in his bureau drawer. Their physical absence modified his impulsive spending behavior, and enabled the Limachers to begin paying off their debt.

Most two-income families with financial problems fall into one or more of three situations: negative cash flow, consumer debt, or insufficient savings for emergencies and nonmonthly expenditures. Identifying where your troubles lie will help you create a solution. Look at the forms you filled out after chapters 5 and 6. You'll need to know your total income; total expenses, both monthly and periodic; total debt; and total monthly savings targets.

Let's look at each of the three financial conditions individually. You may have negative cash flow and consumer debt, but you already have a savings account. Or you may have cash flow and debt under control, but have zero savings. Your current position will drive the development of a workable strategy to correct the problems and achieve your goals.

Negative Cash Flow

Negative cash flow means that outgo exceeds income at the end of each month, and ultimately at the end of each year. You are simply spending more money than you have, and chances are you often have to scramble to find funds to meet annual obligations like auto registration fees, insurance payments, and taxes.

How can this be? How can you spend more money than you really have? Credit. Credit cards, gas cards, car payments, credit lines, finance companies, and other forms of loans have enabled you to live beyond your means. You may not have run out of means yet, but you're probably heading in that direction rapidly. In most cases, negative cash flow is managed by increasing debt each year by the same amount as your annual negative cash flow.

Look at the Carters. Doug and Susie earn $85,000 together, or about $57,000 after taxes. After totaling their monthly and annual expenses, which included car payments, mortgage payments, credit card minimums, utilities, food, clothing, gifts, and personal cash needs, their total expenditures for the year were about $63,000. They were shocked. When we looked at the running balances owed on their credit cards, we found about $6,000 added in the last year. The Carters overspent by $6,000 a year, and that $6,000 showed right up on three credit cards.

Chloe, the Carters' daughter, is an avid skier. Ski equipment and trips are expensive, but the Carters wanted to provide positive reinforcement and allowed her to pursue her interest. Because they let Chloe charge ski equipment on their credit cards, transactions piled up, often before they were aware of them.

Chloe's hobby didn't account for all the additional credit card charges; the Carters tended to use plastic off and on during the month, but toward the end of each pay period, as cash became tight, they used credit more frequently—to tide them over until they received their next paychecks. Looking back over credit card statements, they recognized increased activity around the twelfth to fifteenth and the twenty-seventh to thirty-first of every month.

The Carters

Total Net Monthly Income	$4,750
Total Monthly Expenses	5,250
Operating Expenses	
Fixed	210
Variable	420
Credit Card Minimums	400
Mortgage	2,000
Auto Loan	400
Household	970
Periodic/Nonmonthly	500
One to Four Payments a Year	350
	$5,250
Monthly Cash Flow	$ (500)

Doug and Susie had never considered the concept of negative cash flow as other than an obscure condition that temporarily afflicted businesses, but two-income families can be affected when they spend based on their illusion of wealth.

Gary and Sally Grey had a different experience with negative cash flow. They always managed to have enough money to pay their monthly obligations, but they had to dip into their savings account (which was intended as a down payment on a house) to pay their insurance premiums and taxes. They planned to "pay back" their savings accounts—figuring they were only taking a short-term loan. In reality, their house account would grow by a few thousand dollars and then shrink again when insurance premiums and taxes came due. What happened to the Greys is shown at the top of the next page.

When the Greys started saving money for their house, they agreed to put away $4,800 a year—hoping to stretch it to $5,000—and have enough for a down payment and closing costs on a modest home within four years. They also took into account potential income increases, so that by the fourth year of saving, they expected to set aside about $700 a month.

The Greys' Phantom Savings

Monthly Deposit to House Account	$ 400	
Annual Deposit		$4,800
Annual Insurance Premiums	1,200	
Taxes	2,200	
Total	$3,400	
Net Savings		$1,400

But they failed to factor in their annual expenses—those one to four times a year items—and were becoming increasingly frustrated. The Greys also carried a constant credit card balance of about $2,000. Therefore, instead of saving up to $5,000 a year, they were overspending by $600.

Monthly Deposit to House Account	$ 400	
Annual Deposit		$4,800
Annual Insurance Premiums	1,200	
Taxes	2,200	
Total	$3,400	
Net Savings		$1,400
Annual Credit Card Debt	$2,000	
Net Cash Flow		$ (600)

When they realized they were suffering from negative cash flow, they were surprised but relieved to know what the trouble was.

Dealing with Negative Cash Flow

Despite the anxiety you may feel about your own negative cash flow, take heart. It can be reversed in a number of ways. The path you choose will be the one that best suits your situation. Since each debt load differs in amount and severity, the tactics used to pay it down will vary accordingly. Some people may find that only moderate action is required; others, who have more serious issues, will need a radical plan. The following four phases of action are listed from the simplest and most easily accomplished to complex steps needed to stem extreme negative cash flow. Begin with the phase or phases that you believe will be most effective and then monitor your progress. Implement others as necessary to eliminate all of your negative cash flow.

Reversing Negative Cash Flow: Reduce or Eliminate Expenses

Phase One: Reduce or discontinue operating expenses such as cable television, telephone usage, utilities, dining out, entertainment, parking tickets, clothes, dry cleaning, gifts, and contributions.

Phase Two: Reduce or discontinue other expenses such as house cleaning, gardeners, babysitters or child care, vacations, pet care, and counseling.

Phase Three: Review other set operating expenses; refinance credit card debts to an installment loan over thirty-six to sixty months to reduce amount of monthly debt payments; refinance mortgage to lower monthly payments; sell personal items such as automobiles, motorcycles, boats, recreation vehicles, computers, or stereos; freeze, sell, or discontinue club memberships; look for lower insurance rates for auto, health, disability, and homeowners policies; increase insurance deductibles; total all required operating, debt, and one to four times a year payments, and limit personal expenses to the amount remaining after these expenses are paid.

Phase Four: Consider a major overhaul of your living situation: if renting, move to a home with lower rent; rent out a room in your house; secure private refinancing loans with interest-only payments or with payments to begin a year later; refinance your first mortgage or obtain a second mortgage to consolidate consumer debt and lower monthly debt payments.

While you are reversing your negative cash flow by eliminating expenses, you can also increase your income by implementing the following phases, also in order of severity, for the mildest to the most severe situation.

Reversing Negative Cash Flow: Increase Income

Phase One: If employed, ask for a raise. If self-employed, plan ways to increase your personal income or draw, the money you receive as owner of a sole-proprietor business. If one spouse is not working, consider part-time or full-time work.

Phase Two: If you typically receive a tax refund, check with your tax accountant to determine the proper withholding allowances to increase your exemptions, thereby increasing your take-home pay. This tactic effectively enables you to take your refund in monthly installments rather than as a lump sum once a year.

Other options include temporarily discontinuing voluntary payroll deductions, such as savings plans and retirement plans; considering a second job or looking for ways to make free-lance income; or selling personal items to obtain funds for debt reduction.

Phase Three: If phases one and two are insufficient, consider changing jobs to increase your salary and improve your situation.

The Carters spent $6,000 a year more than they actually had. The task before them was to determine which phase of reducing and eliminating expenses or increasing income would work for them.

When they evaluated the family situation, they determined that most of their problems could be solved in phase one approaches. They reviewed credit card statements to find out how much they actually spent eating out every month, and were surprised to find that they spent about $500 a month in restaurants. Because Chloe was a teenager and their only child, she usually went with them. At first, they thought they could just stop eating out altogether and get rid of their negative cash flow. Then they realized how unrealistic that approach was. They decided to eat out less, cutting back their bill to about $250 a month. In return, each family member took turns cooking dinner.

Their drive to reverse negative cash flow also compelled them to finally cancel the "premium channel" service on their cable. Since they had a VCR, they never watched the pay channels anyway. That saved $20 a month. Chloe's skiing also had to be reconsidered. Instead of skiing almost every weekend, Doug and Susie decided Chloe could ski once or twice a month. They also took back their credit card, thereby eliminating her tendency to spend money on unnecessary new equipment. In the winter months, this meant substantial savings; averaged over twelve months, it saved about $100 a month. They also encouraged Chloe to get an after-school job to pay for her hobby.

Now the Carters' negative cash flow stood at $130. The next item they considered was clothes. Both Susie and Doug liked new clothes, usually taking advantage of sales, but they agreed that they spent too much. When they honestly evaluated what they spent, they realized they were buying new clothes at the rate of $150 a month each, or $300 together. If they stopped buying clothes altogether, they would actually reverse their negative cash flow. But they agreed that that would be unrealistic. Instead, they agreed to spend only $75 a month each—which would include ties, stockings, sportswear, and an occasional blouse or shirt.

These actions reversed the Carters' cash flow, resulting in a positive cash flow of $20 a month. But it generated no surplus for their savings needs. When they looked back over their vacation activities of the previous year, they found they took several airplane trips, often in business class, where few discounts were available. They decided to fly coach, buy their tickets in advance, and even travel by car. By doing so, they freed up another $120 a month, bringing their positive cash flow to $140 a month.

The Carters

Total Net Monthly Income	$4,750
Total Monthly Expenses	4,610
Operating Expenses	
Fixed	190
Variable	320
Credit Card Minimums	400
Mortgage	2,000
Auto Loan	400
Household	720
Periodic/Nonmonthly	230
One to Four Payments a Year	350
	$4,610
Monthly Cash Flow	$140

By arresting their negative cash flow in ways they identified and selected, the Carters accomplished three goals: they took control of their money away from whims and put it to work toward desires; they realized they hardly missed the things they'd been spending so freely on; and they felt good about their financial situation.

The only successful approach to reversing negative cash flow is to act rather than react. Instead of spending and making do with whatever is left over, you work from the top, reviewing how much you spend and deciding what is really necessary. Based on your own decisions, these new values and goals motivate new actions. The key to success is choice.

Debt Elimination

Either you have consumer debt, or you don't. For the purposes of our plan, consumer debt is all outstanding balances over sixty days on credit cards, department store cards, gas cards, medical bills, overdue taxes, and personal loans obtained to consolidate such debts. It also includes loans through finance companies for such purchases as computers, stereos, furniture, musical instruments, and health club memberships. Car loans are not included in the consumer-debt definition because few people pay cash for a new car. We regard a car loan with moderate interest as a three- to five-year family operating expense. However, it can be a pivotal point in reversing negative cash flow.

No matter how you look at it, consumer debt is not desirable. You may believe that everyone has a little consumer debt—that a small credit card balance is no big deal; that financing a large purchase through a finance company is common. Not true. By taking on consumer debt, you agree to pay someone else later for what you want *now*. Credit card interest rates range from about 13 percent (often only if you carry a monthly balance of at least $1,000) to 22 percent. On top of that, many cards charge an annual fee of $20 or more. Before the Tax Reform Act of 1986, you might have been able to justify consumer debt—after all, it was tax deductible. You never got it all back, of course, but it could be a minor source of pleasure to know the government was helping you pay a little of it. But as we know, the government yanked consumer interest deductibility through a phase-out program that was complete at the end of the 1990 tax year.

Look at consumer debt this way. If you continually carry a balance on a credit card charging 17 percent annual interest and are only making minimum payments, every dollar you charged is costing you at least another 17 cents. A $25 book cost $29.25; a $200 dress actually cost you $234—would you have made the purchase at that price? With a $5,000 annual balance, you've spent $850 a year in interest that you could have chosen to save or spend toward your common goals had you paid your balances monthly or not used credit at all. Consumer debt is a prevalent American habit—a symptom of living by default. It precipitates a debt condition that tends to be prolonged, often with increasing debt balances.

Consider the situation of the Jongs. Danny and Carolyn Jong had finally realized their dream—buying a 1920s California bungalow. The two-bedroom house had hardwood floors, plaster walls, lots of windows, a dining room with built-in cabinets, leaded glass, and a quaint gas-equipped kitchen. On their combined income of $75,000, they stretched to buy the $250,000 house. But California real estate had appreciated consistently, often with double-digit annual increases, so the Jongs worried little about the strain. They also counted on salary increases; Carolyn was completing an MBA and had been promised a promotion and a 20-percent raise.

Once they moved into the house, they started working to make it home. In their old apartment, they'd made do with a stereo left over from college. But in the new house they put together an intricate sound system that involved running wires in the crawl space. They bought a new gas range for the kitchen to satisfy their gourmet hobby. And they bought a spa for the backyard because they figured that with all the work they were doing on the house, they'd need to relax. All of their purchases were made in a spirit of playfulness and excitement, backed by a sense of solvency.

Then the Jongs discovered the house needed more work than they had anticipated. A bathroom that they originally thought needed only new paint and fixtures actually required new framing, a result of water damage from old leaky pipes. Instead of $1,000, the job cost closer to $5,000. After the first rain, the Jongs also discovered serious drainage problems. Danny was able to do the repairs himself, but the cost of the materials added up rapidly. When they began converting the basement into a family room, they discovered water damage in the concrete foundation and had to break it out and start over—another cosmetic job turned overhaul.

Suddenly, the Jongs were in debt. A year before they had been relatively cash rich. Now, they were faced with finding ways to finance a new bathroom, a new family room, and new fixtures they couldn't return. They turned to credit. This is what the Jongs' debt sheet looked like:

The Jongs' Debt

Expense	Balance	Debt Vehicle	Interest Rate
Bathroom Work	$ 5,000	Credit Line	15%
Family Room and Foundation Work	8,000	Credit Card Advance	18
Sound System	3,000	Finance Company	22
Stove	2,500	Finance Company	22
Hot tub	1,500	Finance Company	22
Total	$20,000		

The final crunch came when Carolyn's company couldn't give her the promised 20-percent raise when she completed her MBA. A quarterly loss and soft economic times kept her raise at 10 percent, but the couple had already spent as if they had the 20 percent.

There are two ways to eliminate debt—well, three, but we don't count bankruptcy as an alternative here. The Jongs could either pay off their debt monthly in the largest amounts they could afford, or they could consolidate it into a single sum with one level monthly payment. The benefit of consolidating is lower interest rates than credit cards and lower monthly payments. Look for options that provide lower interest rates or lower monthly payments, such as credit union loans, equity loans, low-interest family loans, and employer loans.

With approximately $54,000 in after-tax income, the Jongs had about $4,500 a month to spend. Monthly payments on their new debt quickly soared to $800 a month. After their mortgage payment of $2,500, they had $2,000 to spend on their other expenses—groceries, utilities, clothing, gifts, one car loan, the One to Four Payments a Year account, and the debt they had recently incurred. The Jongs were faced with some spending choices. When they first bought the house, they chose to fix it up as quickly as possible, even if that meant going into debt. As soon as they started paying for structural improvements, their desire to acquire additional furnishings waned. Then, once the repairs were made, the Jongs were driven by the wish to eradicate their debt as quickly as possible.

The Jongs, proud that they had purchased their home with their own money, were reluctant to turn to their families for a loan to pay off their debt. But they realized they had little choice. They were able to borrow $10,000 from Danny's parents at 10 percent, and they added another $5,000 to their 15 percent credit line. Then, they began paying off the loans at about $1,000 a month. It wasn't as quick as they wanted, but it was a start. With one loan and one lower interest rate, they felt less adrift.

Saving: Healthy Habit, Healthy Cash Flow

Just as important as reducing debt is building savings at the same time. Many people begin slashing their debt with the zealousness of Zorro only to be undermined when the holidays, required annual expenses, or emergencies arise. Things go along well for six to eight months as they pay down their debt as quickly as possible. It's a heady feeling to be getting ahead in the game. Suddenly, however, it's Christmas and it seems impossible to really cut back on generosity. So, $1,000 goes back on the credit cards, possibly nearly wiping out all the progress you've made in the last few months. This scenario emphasizes the need to save consistently each month.

The paramount importance of a regular savings plan cannot be overemphasized. Why? First, with money saved in an account designated for bills that come due one to four times a year, you will avoid the dilemma of having no resources to cover a periodic payment such as property taxes. Second, a savings account serves as a barometer to indicate whether or not you can afford to buy or do certain things: clothing, gifts, and travel, for example. You gauge your upcoming needs against the funds in your savings account to determine your actions. Third, a savings account effectively accommodates nonmonthly expenses and enables you to experience peace of mind and confidence.

The failure to save enough money or even to save at all plagues many families, as evidenced by the national average savings rate of 4 percent. On a $60,000 income, 4 percent is $2,400—hardly enough to cover annual sporadic expenses. The problem is compounded by required expenses that compel us to amass $20,000 to $50,000 in consumer debt over three to ten years. Our role model for debt is our own federal government. Most Americans regard themselves as spenders rather than savers, as consumers rather than investors. Developing a savings habit is essential to your overall financial health. Learning to regard yourself as a saver instead of a spender may have the greatest impact on your situation.

One of the most difficult issues we encounter with clients that invariably results from the failure to save or the accumulation of debt is emotional and mental stress. Stress itself then becomes a pressure on top of everything else and manifests itself as anxiety, depression, fear, or anger. If you find yourself in an emotionally charged situation, grant yourself forgiveness and understanding. Most people will encounter some degree of stress with their financial matters, but berating yourself only aggravates an already difficult situation. If you forgive yourself, you will reduce the pressure and regenerate the energy you lost from being upset. Make provisions to nurture and sustain your emotional well-being. Create your own ways of providing inspirations and revitalization. Be supportive of each other as you go through the activities of the plan, creating new healthier conditions and habits.

Always be as patient and compassionate as you can in addressing financial issues. Countless magazine surveys have found that more people fight about money than any other topic. So, don't get too frustrated when you do reach impasses. You will work through them. The fact that you've agreed to pursue a plan of attack together and have agreed on common goals indicates that you can work together. So hang in there.

What to Do with a Windfall

Sometimes you're the beneficiary of a lump sum of cash—maybe a Christmas bonus, a family gift, or your tax refund. What do you do with it? Take a great vacation, buy new furniture, throw a party, use it all to pay down your debt? We recommend you think first: in the designed, balanced approach to the use of your money, your feelings, motivations, and goals are key criteria in all spending decisions—not just your ordinary income.

We recommend that you use any windfall in a balanced way. Make your choices carefully to achieve a number of results. We're not suggesting that you go out and spend it on a vacation, or buy that Harley you've teased your spouse about since you met. Instead, consider your financial obligations and desires and use the money to further each of your objectives. Put some of the money in one or more of the four savings accounts we outlined in chapter 6, use some of it to reduce debt, and then give yourself a little treat, acknowledging that the biggest treat is in eliminating debt and putting money into a savings account.

Kara Little received a $5,000 bonus after her company reached its fifth anniversary of profitability. Kara had been with the company since its inception ten years before and had been loyal through the lean times. Kara and her husband, Tim, were trying to pay off a $7,000 credit card debt, and had begun building their savings accounts, but had been able to contribute little to the reserve account. Kara wanted to sign over the bonus check to the bank and watch their debt melt away. Tim thought they should put some of the bonus into their savings, but he also felt Kara deserved a reward for her hard work over the years. Kara didn't think it was necessary.

We suggested they do a bit of everything they had mentioned. The Littles put $2,250 toward the credit card debt and $2,250 toward the savings accounts. That left $500 for a personal treat. They decided to do something they'd both enjoy and remember for a long time. With cash, they went to see *Les Misérables*, had an after-theater dinner in one of the city's best restaurants, and spent the night in a cozy European-style hotel—all on Kara's company. When they went home the next day—all of ten miles away—they felt fulfilled. They'd paid off some debt, padded their savings accounts, and enjoyed a romantic night out without worrying about how they were going to pay for it—something they hadn't done in years.

Setting Up Your Action Plan

Now that you've read about other people's successes, it's time to claim those feelings of confidence, direction, and accomplishment for yourself. Essentially, you've been given a second shot at taking control of your financial situation and guiding yourself toward the feelings and conditions that you want, rather than those that are thrust upon you by external forces. This shift will require that you change your habits—that you learn to become a saver rather than a spender. The process requires honesty, both with yourselves individually and with each other. You must be specific, and not give in to the tendency to gloss over uncomfortable "details" such as clothing or furnishings.

New habits take time, but if you keep yourself focused on your motivations and common goals, you will succeed. Establishing your savings accounts will help you get started; as you fund those accounts your habits will begin to change. With proper savings, the property tax or auto insurance bill won't be cause for concern and anxiety.

The two greatest areas for addressing action are your negative cash flow and your consumer debt. Negative cash flow can be eradicated through one or more phases of cutting expenses— from canceling premium cable service to selling a home that is too expensive—or increasing income—from changing your withholding to getting a new job. As you reverse your negative cash flow, you also can begin to eliminate debt. You may need to consolidate debt into one loan to pay off at a lower interest rate over a longer period, or you may need to sell that expensive car you wanted so badly before identifying your burning desires.

To set up your own family cash flow plan, use the charts and information you compiled at the end of chapter 6. You have some choices to make: you need to determine how much you *want* to spend on certain items, and how much you can *afford* to spend, taking into consideration the requirements of each of the four savings accounts. You may encounter some troubles along the way—emotional or financial. Remember that you are working together for your common goals, and learn to support each other more actively. Together you can take control of your spending and have what it is you want—security, a new house, a dream vacation.

‖‖ CHECKPOINT 7 ‖‖

Taking control of your finances often means making spending choices. Most two-income families suffer from negative cash flow, heavy consumer debt, and/or lack of savings.

Negative cash flow can be reversed by cutting costs and/or increasing income.

To eradicate consumer debt, you may need to combine your debt into one loan with a lower interest rate, lower payments, or flexible payment terms. Low-interest family loans, credit union loans, and employer or business loans are options.

To begin building savings, you need to identify annual and monthly expenses and other cash needs and begin to set aside money each month.

1. Determine whether or not you have negative cash flow by comparing your grand total on the Expense Guide you worked on following chapter 6 with your monthly income, computed on the following page.

Total Net Monthly Income	$_____
Monthly Expenses	
Operating Expenses	
Fixed	_____
Variable	_____
Household Expenses	_____
Debt Payments	_____
Periodic/Nonmonthly	_____
One to Four Payments a Year	_____
Reserve	_____
Investments/Major Purchases	_____
Total Monthly Expenses	$_____
Monthly Cash Remaining	$_____

2. Discuss the four phases of reversing negative cash flow to identify the approach that will work best for you.

3. Discuss how you can increase your income using the three phases outlined earlier in this chapter.

8

Working Together

Up to this point, we have talked mainly about adjusting spending priorities and cutting costs, and it may sound as if stabilizing your financial situation means giving up the good life forever. Even the words *cutting costs* may sound altogether too Spartan for the affluent, comfortable lives you are used to living. But this is a plan meant to achieve your goals, the dreams you have chosen as crucial to you and your future happiness. We don't advocate dull living; we want you to live lives that are exciting and fulfilling. But when we talk about cutting costs, we are also talking about realizing your goals, and the stronger and more interesting your goals are, the more likely they are to motivate change.

In establishing goals, aim for burning desires; don't settle for weak wishes. When you really want something, you are willing to do whatever it takes to see the result. But you must always keep the goal in sight. Try not to say: "Something is being taken away from me"; or "I have to give something up." Instead, remember what it is you really want—and how much closer you are to having it once you take charge of your money. As you do, your energy, attitudes, and emotions will shift, and you will start to be results driven. Your new attitude will be: "I'm not giving something up, I'm getting something I really want." You will begin to spend according to your desires rather than your old spending style and habits as this genuine shift in motivations and payoffs comes alive.

We've emphasized the importance of setting goals and the role they play in rethinking your finances and your spending choices. The first thing to remember about a two-income family is that you may be a couple and a family, but you are two individuals. You aren't going to agree on everything, and you are probably going to have some different motivations. Your differences may be partly why you were attracted to each other in the first place, and there's no reason for you to have relinquished your separate identities when you married. On the other hand, your similarities and like interests are also part of what drew, and keeps, you together. We focus on these similarities because they generate your primary common goals. But there will also be room for give-and-take and individual dreams and achievements. The success of one or the other in any endeavor will contribute health and inspiration.

Great Minds Think Alike

Your two minds may think in similar ways, but not in exactly the same way—you already know that from having been together for any stretch of time. Diverging opinions fuel most family arguments, from how to drive a car to what to have for dinner. But now it's time to explore even further ways in which you *do* think alike.

Begin with an open mind—but preferably behind closed doors. Go to separate rooms with a pad and pencil, set a time limit, and each make a list of the three family goals you really desire, in order of importance. Bear in mind that their importance can fluctuate. Your primary concern is to identify your top three goals, regardless of their order. Then compare your lists.

Chances are your lists won't overlap on everything; in fact, you may share only one point. If your lists are completely different, don't despair. Explore the essence of what you really want and you may discover how they are alike in context. The point is to list *realistic* burning desires. As we said earlier, unrealistic dreams remain dreams. Realistic dreams can become realities.

Once your common goals are set and you begin to work to achieve them, consider your individual goals—goals your partner cannot or does not want to share. To feel satisfied and happy, you cannot completely ignore your separate desires even while working toward the common ones. You must address your individual goals, even if only to agree that they are goals, then create mutually acceptable provisions for them so that you can turn your energy toward the shared goals. Keep individual goals in mind so that you both benefit from their achievement, too.

Battle of the Budget

To say that Scott and Megan Cannon were not communicating would be an understatement. They were financially comfortable on $80,000 a year. Scott earned $55,000 as a medical equipment salesperson, and Megan earned about $25,000 as a chiropractic assistant. They had been married almost a decade, but for the last few years they had been fighting constantly about money. No financial calamity loomed on their horizon, but they bickered over how money should be spent, arguing not only about who should pay the bills each month, but how the bills should be paid. They argued over how money should be used: Should they carry a balance on a credit card in order to build up their savings? Should they pay with cash, or was it better to use credit so they didn't have to carry around a lot of cash or the checkbook? They fought about the necessity of various expenditures, like a housekeeper or cab fares. In short, the Cannons' financial life was very volatile.

In other ways, the couple got along fine. They enjoyed each other's company, shared athletic and cultural interests, and agreed largely on politics, religion, and sexual values. The Cannons couldn't figure out why they were constantly feuding about money, but whenever the mention of money, income, expenditures, and long-term savings came up, Scott and Megan went at each other. They were unhappy, but felt unable to resolve it themselves. They considered going to see a marriage counselor, but decided instead that a money problem should be handled by money people. In reality, theirs was both a money and an emotional problem. When they presented their situation to us, the key to solving the mystery came when we asked them to discuss their goals. They were astounded to discover that the root of their problems came from a basic misunderstanding of each other's dreams, particularly regarding money and the use of it.

Hard-line Tactics

After seven years of marriage, Scott desperately wanted to buy a house. He was tired of renting and envied friends and colleagues who were renovating their own homes. He also resented living in a place in which he could do no major refurbishing. The goal of buying a house even affected his spending habits. He ate out less often, he stopped buying new athletic shoes every other month, and he starched his own shirts. To Scott, owning a home was the final hurdle to becoming an adult. He grew up in a spacious suburban home in the 1950s and 1960s, and having a house meant security and position. The only problem was that Megan didn't seem to share his passion.

In Scott's traditional family, his father commuted forty minutes to work each day while his mother stayed home with the kids. As the kids got older, his mother worked as a volunteer but managed to be home when they returned from school. His dad handled all the family finances, and his mom received a "house allowance" to take care of the basic family needs. Old-fashioned? Unfair? Maybe. But at least it worked. Scott didn't think he would want to be a husband in control of the family finances, but he sometimes joked that his and Megan's money

troubles would be over if he took complete control of their finances. The comment, though not serious, often got him hostile looks from Megan.

When Scott and Megan first got married they talked a lot about buying a house, how they would fix it up, what they liked and disliked in the way of interior design. But in the last few years the constructive talk about goals had been driven out by arguments over money. Because every discussion about money ended in a quarrel, Scott was reluctant to bring up the house. Instead he continued to be as frugal as possible, occasionally suggesting ways they could save money. If they kept saving, he figured, they could afford the house in another year.

Unspoken Wishes

When Megan graduated from college, she went on the professional golf circuit. She lived tournament to tournament, out of a suitcase much of the time, staying in other people's homes and in hotel rooms. She loved the nomadic life and the thrill of playing some of the best courses in the country. She had her share of media attention one year as an upstart young golfer. She had even had the ultimate recognition: her parents had seen her interviewed on television after she shot an astonishing eagle on a hole that more established golfers finished with only birdies. For the most part, though, Megan barely made a sufficient living and knew she would never be a top professional golfer. It was enough to play golf and get paid for something she had fun doing, but she knew deep inside that it was temporary.

So, as the years went by, she began to yearn for a more predictable life—to get married, have a house of her own, start a family. Aggravating the situation was a chronic problem with her back from a pinched nerve she had developed in college. She had been seeing a chiropractor in efforts to alleviate pain, and she'd always been pleased with the results. So, when she retired from golf after six years on the road, she started working as a chiropractic assistant. She had never considered a "real" career, so working for a chiropractor seemed only logical.

About a year after she retired, Megan met Scott on a golf course. He was out "whacking balls," as he called it, on the municipal driving range. During their courtship, Megan talked about her desire to settle down after having been on tour for so many years. Scott shared her desire to settle down, which began to develop into the dream of owning their own home. But in the last couple of years, Megan had begun to feel uncomfortable about her career situation, unlike Scott, who had settled into his work. Megan was thirty-four and making $25,000 as an assistant to someone else. Her golf friends were either still golfing or in golf-related jobs. Her friends from college were beginning to get *vice-president* printed on their business cards. Megan felt left behind.

One day it dawned on her. Why be a chiropractic assistant forever? There was no reason she couldn't become a chiropractor herself. She was certainly bright enough, and she actually relished the thought of going back to school full time. She began to dream and think about it daily. She mentioned her plan to Scott a couple of times but got a lukewarm response, something like: "Well, after we get the house, maybe you could do that." She acquiesced silently. The idea of going to school did seem rather unrealistic. After all, the house was the dream they'd been talking about for years.

Over time, Megan resigned herself to putting off her goal until they bought the house. After they became accustomed to making mortgage payments, maybe she could start saving money for school. Occasionally, she mentioned her desire to go back to school, but she felt it was ultimately selfish and let it go. However, the unspoken frustration led to continuing arguments about money.

Learning to Communicate

The Cannons' money spats erupted from a lack of communication. Scott was either unable or unwilling to recognize that Megan's goal was realistic. His eyes were still set on the house; she, in turn, was dissatisfied and building resentment.

In the end, Scott was "winning" because they were saving money for the house, and Megan was "losing" because her goal was still in the dream stage and nothing was being done about it. Unconsciously, Megan had started looking for ways in which she could "win," other than asserting her wishes and beginning to save money toward school. The housekeeper was a perfect example. For $100 a month, Megan hired a helper to clean the apartment once a week. The couple didn't need help cleaning such a small space, but by telling Scott they should have a housekeeper and then hiring her, Megan chalked up a point.

When they sat down to identify their mutual goals, the Cannons realized something that surprised them both. Scott and Megan each wanted the other to achieve his or her dream. Scott's major desire was to buy a house, while Megan listed a house and chiropractic school. The overlap, of course, was the house. But the exercise also helped Scott realize just how strongly Megan wanted to go to school. Until he saw Megan's list in black and white, he hadn't understood how serious she was.

He also understood that Megan shared his dream. When he realized that she was not out to defeat him by throwing away their savings, Scott softened his Spartan economic stance. For the first time, he began to listen and care about Megan's dream. For her part, Megan realized that she did still feel strongly about owning a home. As Scott began to accept her wish to become a chiropractor, she began to accept more openly his need to have a house. They began to communicate and share their aspirations—just as they had when they first started dating. Over time and a few more arguments—no one changes over-night—they finally agreed to a solution to accomplish both goals.

Up to this point, the couple had been stashing their excess monthly cash flow in a savings account for the house. They agreed that the primary goal was still the house, but a strong second was Megan's schooling. Because Megan's goal had been ignored for so long, however, they agreed to make it a priority and slow down saving for the house. Pursuing a common goal requires some give-and-take from each spouse. Scott accepted that it would take longer to buy the house, and Megan agreed to continue working part time while she went to school.

They diverted some of the house account funds to the school account, and they found some places to trim expenditures to unearth more cash for their savings needs. Because Megan finally saw progress being made toward her primary goal, she agreed that the housekeeper was unnecessary. Together, they agreed to cut their entertainment spending and start reading aloud to each other—a no-expense pastime they used to enjoy.

The Cannons' Savings Plan

	BEFORE AGREEMENT		AFTER AGREEMENT	
	Savings	Expenses	Savings	Expenses
House	$800/month		$600	
School	0		$400	
Housekeeper		$100		0
Entertainment		$500		$400

Discussing their goals introduced a new openness and exploration into their relationship, and they were able to move forward together at last. Like the Cannons, you can achieve common and individual desires—if you understand each other's dreams and work together toward mutual satisfaction.

Courtesy and Consideration

Often when couples argue about money, the concept of "rights" arises. People who work hard to earn money often feel it is their right to buy things to satisfy themselves—from hobby supplies and tickets to cultural events to clothing—without the consent or even knowledge of their partners. We prefer not to see the notion of "rights" applied in a marriage because it sparks confrontation. A marriage is an arrangement of love and equality entered into freely; we suggest that instead of demanding financial rights, you and your spouse exercise courtesy and consideration in recognizing each other's wishes and desires.

Many couples have trouble balancing intimacy—blending their personalities—with etiquette—recognizing and respecting each other's individuality. No doubt this balance was simpler in the days when marriages were arranged and financially established by the spouses' families. Business partnerships were forged as marital bonds were tied, and couples knew that their relationship had different aspects. When you and your spouse talk about money, remember that you have entered into a partnership with someone you really care about—and who cares about you. Be polite and generous, not defensive and suspicious—and you will find that your partner will respond in kind. Long-lasting marriages, like long-lasting relationships of any kind, are founded on mutual respect. Even if you believe that your husband or wife has no idea how to handle money, you are both trying to learn more about finances—that is why you are working together to improve your financial situation.

Logistics

Things don't run by themselves, so you will need to determine who should be responsible for what. One way to nurture a courteous approach to money and to stick to your plan for your finances is to assign tasks by mutual agreement. Having specific responsibilities will minimize misunderstandings and make your financial workings more efficient. You can outline your responsibilities in a number of ways, but the key is assessing each spouse's level of comfort and competence with certain tasks.

One approach we have found helpful is to consider yourselves a team. As team members, you have individual positions, such as head of planning and head of operations. Assign tasks based on your abilities. If one of you is good at planning the big picture, that person should be head of planning. If one of you is good with numbers and is well organized, that person should be the operations head. Here are the basics of each job:

Head of Planning

Assemble data
Verify accuracy and thoroughness of data
Plan payment schedules
Plan savings needs
Prioritize tasks on a time line
Regularly review results and fine-tune strategy

Head of Operations

Make deposits and transfers
Write checks
Balance family checking and savings accounts
Generate monthly reports
Maintain organized files

If you use the team approach, you may sometimes share or exchange roles. This can make carrying out your plan more interesting and interactive. Grant each other the time to develop the necessary skills and habits that will aid you in your successful financial management. Be creative; the point is to decide together what your individual tasks will be. Set up a system any way you want, but set it up.

Two-Income Etiquette

Despite your good intentions, some misunderstandings may arise as you try to determine exactly how to manage your two incomes. These guidelines might help you decide how to manage some common problems.

Should we be able to dispose of our individual incomes as we choose? We advocate pooling your money, with separate allowances for each of you to spend at will on such things as lunches, personal entertainment, dry cleaning, transportation, and other incidentals. Sit down together and begin with some estimates of your cash needs. If you have no idea, jot down some ballpark figures, then keep track of what you spend for a month until you have a better estimate. Provide yourselves with that "allowance" either monthly or semimonthly.

An alternative to total pooling is to pool funds required for basic household operations, such as rent or mortgage, utilities, groceries, telephone, cable television, and so forth. This option works best if you both earn approximately the same amount. After contributing half of the household operating costs, including savings, you are free to spend the rest on discretionary items.

If one of you does some work on the side and feels entitled to whatever is earned outside of the regular job, you might divide the extra cash, keeping half and pooling the rest. If your spouse has to work on a Saturday to earn extra money and skips certain chores, you might take over those responsibilities for the day. The point is to operate as a team, taking each other's emotional needs and goals into account.

Should we have separate checking and savings accounts? Joint property is a big issue. Again, we recommend joint accounts, unless one of you travels a great deal. You may want to have two checking accounts—one for bills and one for personal and family needs. Most people also have a joint savings account, but if you have separate goals, as was the case with the Cannons, you might want to have separate accounts.

Couples who had established their own financial identities before getting married may want to retain individual accounts and then contribute an agreed upon amount to a joint account. In this case, two defined financial identities come together to create a third. There would be some pooling and some separation.

The drawback to separate accounts is that you might waste money overspending by not having a common goal and a system of "checks" on your potential self-indulgence. Pooling creates a team approach. Not only do you save money, you gain the power of united effort, as well as streamlining management tasks.

If you do maintain joint accounts, you may want to consider what to do if you divorce. No one wants to plan for this, of course, but two of every three marriages today end in divorce. So, agreement on financial matters can be very important. Some couples write prenuptial agreements or other contracts, but these detract from the air of courtesy, and we believe consideration is of paramount importance to a marriage.

Should we share expenses on a pro rata basis? Not necessarily. If you're pooling your money and one of you makes three times as much as the other one, the higher earning partner is making a larger contribution. For those who choose not to pool all of their funds, a fifty-fifty approach usually works best.

Should major financial decisions be made jointly? Yes, keeping in mind the common primary goal you have determined. The answer to this question seems obvious, but it's amazing how decision making can be skewed by circumstance. Case in point: Kirsten Emerson wanted her husband, Brian, to know how much she cared about him and how proud she was of the job he was doing. In their marriage Brian was considered the breadwinner and Kirsten, the "cakewinner." His income could have supported them comfortably, but she wanted to work. One day she emptied the couple's savings account—$10,000—to buy Brian a Rolex watch. He had always wanted one, and because the couple was doing so well financially, Kirsten thought he should have it. They weren't saving for anything else in particular, and Kirsten figured that Brian hadn't bought one for himself because he didn't want to be selfish. She presented the watch to him one Friday after work, and Brian nearly lost control. He wasn't doing as well in his job as Kirsten thought. In fact, he knew he might even be losing his job, but he hadn't panicked because they had $10,000 in savings to tide them over. Fortunately, Kirsten's impulsive purchase finally forced Brian to tell her the truth, and they were able to return the watch.

Should daily money decisions be made jointly? No. Doing so would result in endless confusion. To simplify things, appoint certain daily chores, such as dropping off the dry cleaning or doing the grocery shopping, to one of you.

What if one partner makes a purchase over the agreed

limit, or in a category you jointly agreed not to spend money on? Take a deep breath, set aside your assumptions, and together clarify what specifically happened—the amount and nature of the purchase. Once you have the facts, determine how the purchase should be dealt with. For example, you may decide to return the item, select a tradeoff from your cash flow plan to replace the funds, or consider the purchase a gift for an upcoming birthday.

What if your partner does not choose to participate in this plan? In creating and implementing this plan, acknowledge your spouse's feelings and preferences; indicate your willingness to accept his or her position; request a trial period of six months using the plan; discuss ways in which he or she would be willing to participate.

What if one of you continually fails to perform? At the beginning of the plan, establish a written agreement of your roles and responsibilities. Include a provision so that if either party insufficiently completes his or her tasks, that person agrees to relinquish those tasks to the other.

There are so many other financial questions that arise. How should we handle them? We recommend that you obtain referrals for professionals who are qualified to answer your questions, then we highly recommend you verify their competence with references you call. These needs arise most frequently: wills, estate planning, insurance, retirement planning, college education funds, investment advice, prenuptial agreements, ownership of assets and debt, and tax issues. The following professionals should be capable of assisting you with any one or more of the above concerns: certified public accountant (CPA); certified financial planner (CFP); chartered life underwriter (CLU), estate planning attorneys, tax attorneys, family law attorneys, and investment specialists.

Consider these answers and suggestions as broad guidelines rather than as final recommendations. You will have to work out the approach that best suits your personalities. The key is to talk about these things, making an effort to understand each other's perspectives and to respect each other's ideas and sug-gestions. Make these decisions together, even if you will ulti-mately act on them individually.

You are individuals and will have individual goals. The key is to determine where your goals agree and to identify your primary common goal. From there you can identify and begin to work toward each other's individual aspirations. The key is courtesy, consideration, and a willingness to support your individual and mutual goals.

To manage your two-income family, together assign individ-ual tasks for specific family needs and responsibilities. You may want to choose a head of planning and a head of operations. It doesn't matter how you set up your family management, but you should do it. Review your efforts and results regularly, preferably monthly.

1. Review your individual and common goals. Individually, in separate rooms, write down your three top goals. Try not to second-guess what your spouse is writing in the other room. Then come back to compare what you've written, seeing what your mutual aims and individual pursuits are.

2. Go back over the strategies in chapter 7 for reversing neg-ative cash flow. Now that you've more realistically deter-mined your goals, remember that you are not being asked to *give up* anything. You are *choosing* to trim spending on relatively unimportant things in order to *get* what you really want. Now, identify areas in which you can trim and start saving. Start monitoring yourselves to verify that you've achieved these goals.

3. Determine your financial roles. Who has the affinity for the following tasks and responsibilities?

- Keep track of bills for payment and write checks
- Establish savings needs and goals
- Maintain accurate balance in checkbook register
- Maintain files for receipts, bank statements
- Generate monthly reports
- Make adequate deposits to correct accounts
- Determine long-term financial needs

Realize that not all families will have a natural head of planning or head of operations. Divide the tasks to best take advantage of natural abilities. Don't volunteer for something that you know your spouse has more talent for. And, if one party is totally incapable of keeping track of finances, you can jointly provide the person who does the financial work with a gratuity of sorts. For example, if one of you agrees to take care of all the finances, the other one can agree to do more of the household chores. Again, you'll do well to keep in mind courtesy and consideration—a real willingness to help out.

9

Long-term Success

ince money, and issues relating to money, cut across so many levels—from the most basic transactions to our deepest feelings about ourselves— understanding your feelings and communicating with your spouse is crucial. Although we are inevitably linked to the lessons we learned in childhood about money and behavior, we can change. Emotions motivate our actions, and recognizing what we want most will help us achieve it. But we also need to understand the actual nitty-gritty of our financial situation. You must decide what you want out of life and then figure out your finances: your income, your expenses, your assets and liabilities. Then put the two together, forging a plan that takes into consideration your aspirations and dreams and the bottom line. If you are honest with yourself, the emotional side and the practical side will merge.

Many of us become catatonic when we see our own accounts—even if we manage complex budgets at work. We just don't want to think about money, although we may feel entitled to spend as we like. Whether this reluctance (and in some cases paralyzing anxiety) comes from fear, rebellion, a wish to be taken care of, or simply boredom, most people have felt it at one time or another. If you've accepted our plan and have done the paperwork, you have overcome that hurdle. The good news is that the more you assume responsibility for managing your money, the more it becomes part of your daily life, and the less time you spend worrying about it. As you free up that energy for other things, you'll have the cash and the determination to do them.

It would be easy to set this book down and say: "Okay, we've learned quite a bit already, and we see some things we'd like to accomplish, so if we just keep our minds on it, we'll do all right." If you say that, however, chances are that you may let the enthusiasm of the moment fade into complacency and slip back into your old habits. Here are some tips on how to keep the plan vital:

Keeping with the Plan

Focus. People often squander money and energy because they feel their true desires are hopeless; reviewing your goals regularly and thinking of your finances as a whole will make it easier for you to determine if you really want another compact disc or a new pair of shoes to add to the stack in your closet.

Talk. We also suggest you keep a schedule; plan to meet together once a month to review your cash flow plan and reassess your goals, and twice a month to pay bills. These meetings will help you practice new habits and stay abreast of developments. In addition, they will foster sustained focus on your goals. The more consistently you maintain attention on your goals, the more likely you are to achieve them. But don't think that if three meetings are good, four or five would be better. Too often, people start the plan with such enthusiasm that they are driven to pay bills as soon as they receive them or start looking for ways midmonth to raise an additional $200 to apply to a credit card balance. With finances constantly on their minds, they burn out quickly.

Most of us are used to planning, directing, and attending meetings in our daily business lives; use the same standards at home. If your children are involved in the family finances, whether they shop for groceries or their own clothes, include them so they can begin to learn about managing money. They need to learn, and they're not likely to find out in school. Select a regular time for your monthly planning session—the third Sunday of the month at four o'clock, for example. Don't choose ten o'clock on a Tuesday night when you're stressed and tired— you have already been in enough meetings at work. Don't wait until you have a "free moment." If you do, you'll be surprised by how busy you are. Make it an official meeting with an agenda, if that helps. Regardless of the format, plan to spend about an hour together. Don't expect to gab for an hour, though. There are some specifics to cover.

Monthly Planning Session

Assess your gains. Consider what you said you would do at the last meeting and whether you did it. Suppose you said you would put $400 in your savings account. Did it get there? Maybe, like the Cannons, you said you'd let the housekeeper go. Did you? You decided to spend $100 less on eating out each month. What happened? You said you'd retire four credit cards. Did you cut them up?

Remember to assess your wins, not evaluate how you did. When you make a decision that requires a specific action, like retiring four credit cards, there's no way to determine "how you did." It's not a *how* kind of question. It's a *yes or no* question. Answer truthfully; don't hedge. As you discuss your progress, try to understand what forces and conditions directed these achievements—what were the dynamics of your actions? These insights will reinforce your actions as you move forward.

Recognize your setbacks. You're going to encounter setbacks, and it's important to acknowledge them in your meeting. If you ignore them now, they will build up until you are forced to see them; by then they may be so overwhelming they will scare you from proceeding with the plan. Remember it's okay to make mistakes—it's human. Perhaps you said you'd spend $600 for food, but you spent $875. Or you said you'd let the housekeeper go, but you didn't. Maybe you did cancel the housekeeper, but with the money you "saved" you hired a personal trainer. Maybe you paid off one credit card, but added to another. These are setbacks, but they're not bells of doom. Instead of chastising yourself and feeling guilty, acknowledge the setback, forgive yourself, and start again. Try to determine why you experienced the setback—was it the result of an emotional or logistical force, or was it an emergency that you could not have foreseen? Whatever the cause, examine what you could have done differently. These experiences will help you choose a more positive action next time.

Set new goals. Unrealistic goals might also cause setbacks. Perhaps eating on $600 a month is impossible. Redefine your family cash flow plan to include $700 for food. It's not a failure; it's a required adjustment. But be honest with yourself; are you spending extra money on something like boned chicken breasts because it's a bother boning them yourself?

You may find you would like to accomplish something in the short term that your family cash flow plan does not account for because that something was an unknown variable when you set up the plan. First conclude together that the desire is worth making changes elsewhere in your plan, then evaluate the situation to see how you can accommodate the extra expense. A month before their youngest son's birthday, Tim and Jill Gladden decided that they really wanted to get him a portable stereo. They hadn't intended to buy him a stereo, but they realized how much he wanted one. In years past, they would have used a credit card; this time, however, they developed a plan to find a way to afford the stereo in cash. They decided to eat out less that month.

Maybe you have been particularly stressed at work and really need some time away from everything, but a weekend getaway isn't part of your plans. One way to create a mini-vacation is to cut corners elsewhere. If you make a lot of long-distance phone calls every month, try cutting back. Write letters instead and save $50 on your phone bill. Choose to replace dinner out or concert tickets with what you really need—to get away. As you begin to spend in accord with your plan so that it becomes almost second nature, you'll discover clever ways to obtain what you want without upsetting the flow of the plan or your commitment to it. Make it a challenge to come up with creative ways to reach those achievements.

In order to keep the plan flexible and dynamic, work with it regularly. Things change, and you have to be prepared to change with them. Having a monthly planning meeting keeps communication and goals fresh. If you don't meet regularly, you risk losing the momentum you've generated. This kind of discipline is critical in the beginning—after all you are planting and nurturing new habits.

Rewards. Most of us respond well to rewards. Like the legendary Pavlovian dogs, we work for treats. So, treat yourself after your monthly meetings. Base your reward on your gains for the month. When the Millers started saving money, they kept a percentage for a treat. If they saved $300, they took $30. Sometimes they spent the $30 on a special Sunday brunch. Sometimes they saved it for bigger rewards. Once they saved their reward for four months in a jar in their closet, and then had a weekend at an inexpensive country inn. Getting a reward brings out the child in a person, and that's good. Once you've begun taking responsibility for your finances, you deserve the perquisites.

Useful Tools

Get into the habit of viewing things related to your finances not as bewildering obligations or tedious chores but as stepping stones to help you realize your dreams. We've designed the Expense Guide and the Primary Motivations and Payoffs chart to help you build your designed money plan, and there are some other tools you might find useful.

Progress charts. Simple visual games can make following the plan more fun and your results more tangible. Like a community fund-raising project that erects a thermometer chart to monitor progress, you can keep track of your family savings plan with a chart on the refrigerator. As you deposit money into your savings accounts every month, color in another block on the chart and watch your money grow. Or, if you're involved in a debt elimination project, use a graph to mark the declining credit card balance. Most people perform better in an atmosphere of fun and excitement. We suggest you create charts, graphs, pictures, or collages to stimulate enthusiasm. The following are examples:

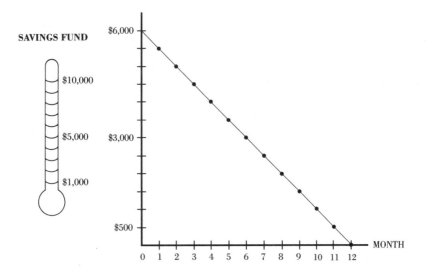

Filing system. Every family, whether they have one income or two, should have a filing system for its finances. Keep your monetary files separate from other information, and make them accessible and easy to use. This is what should be contained in your filing system:

- Receipts (one file for deductible, one for nondeductible)
- Checking/Savings Statements (a separate file for each account)
- Credit Card Data: agreements and card numbers
- Insurance Policies/Claims (a separate file for each policy)
- Financial Statements
- Loan Documents
- Service Agreements/Warranties
- Contracts and Agreements: service providers, leases, and so on (a separate file for each contract)
- Investments (a separate file for each investment)
- Canceled Checks (one file for each account)

Cash flow binder. If visuals make your job easier, consider making a binder for your plan, using the charts and guides outlined in this book. By keeping it all in one location, the plan will be easier to manage.

Included in the binder should be:

- Primary Motivations and Payoffs
- Income Statements (three)
- Expense Guide
- Debts and Liabilities
- Financial Statement
- Insurance Summary

Reading list. Here are some books that might be of extra help in reassessing your family's finances and goals.

Hill, Napoleon. *Think and Grow Rich.* New York: Fawcett Crest, 1960.

Robbins, Anthony. *Unlimited Power.* New York: Ballantine
    Books, 1986.
Roman, Sanaya, and Duane Packer. *Creating Money.* Tiburon,
    Calif: H. J. Kramer, 1988.
Phillips, Michael. *The Seven Laws of Money.* New York: Word
    Wheel and Random House, 1974.
Hall, Mary Bowen. *More for Your Money.* Boston: Houghton
    Mifflin, 1981.

Magazines good for basic financial information and inspiration
by example are *Money* and *Success.*

On Guard for Pitfalls

No matter how organized and dedicated you are, how fancy the
charts on your refrigerator door are, or how certain you are of
your goals, you will encounter problems along the way. But do
not get discouraged. You can't predict every event in the future,
but you can learn how to respond to the unexpected. There will
be surprises that throw off your plan, but there is no need to
throw away the plan because of them.

Sometimes emotional troubles hold us up. Even the most
dedicated followers of the plan can wake up one morning feeling
miserable without knowing why. If this happens, chances are
you've lost sight of your goal. Go over your Primary Motivations
and Payoffs chart and your goals, and remind yourself of the
reason you began the program. Take time to refocus, to rekindle
the fire that got you started in the first place. Everyone gets
depressed, but if you take these mood shifts in stride, you'll
defuse their impact on your progress.

One of the most common pitfalls is the unconscious fear of
success, which is often followed by equally unconscious efforts
to sabotage progress. Tom and Lori Stack were trying to save
money and pay off debt to prepare for their goal, which was to
have a baby. The couple had slashed their debt substantially
when out of the blue they decided to take a European vacation.
They had gotten a good deal on airline tickets, and the whole

trip would cost them $5,000. They had $2,500 in savings and figured they'd let the rest ride on the credit cards.

Fortunately, before they committed themselves to anything they realized they were about to undermine their plan. As they talked about their progress, Lori discovered she was panicked at the prospect of motherhood. The trip symbolized their carefree, impulsive existence. Tom also confessed to getting cold feet about having a baby. But after several long and intense conversations, they reaffirmed their goal and carried on. Like the Stacks, you will undoubtedly have second thoughts, but if you use these constructively to prompt a second or third look, you will be able to adapt new ideas to create a new plan. Reevaluation is an effective tool that can serve to strengthen rather than weaken commitment.

Some pitfalls cannot be avoided. As the Millers made progress toward financial security, they experienced a family emergency they could neither have foreseen nor prevented. Beverly's grandmother in England died, and Beverly needed to accompany her mother to England for the funeral and to take care of other arrangements. The airfare alone cost Beverly $3,000; other expenses racked up another $1,500.

Beverly was understandably upset about her grandmother's death; David, although sympathetic, had never known Beverly's grandmother and focused instead on the blow to the couple's finances. As he struggled emotionally with this setback, his first reaction was to abandon the plan. They had charged Beverly's airline tickets because they didn't have the cash, raising their credit card debt dramatically. The Millers had been keeping charts on their refrigerator door, happily watching their savings swell and their debt diminish. The next month, savings sank and debt deepened. David felt guilty about his lack of empathy for Beverly, but still resented the way "her problem" had slowed down their progress in the plan.

When events like these occur, and they may, stay calm. Accept setbacks as part of the process, take a deep breath, and start again the next month. Too many people treat temporary crises as permanent conditions. Just because the Millers had to spend $3,000 on airline tickets did not mean they had to surrender their goal of being financially secure. Their timetable changed, but their goal was intact.

What people who live by default consider emergencies, people who live by design recognize as mere irritations—hurdles, not roadblocks. Liz Davis and Max Carberry, the couple whose challenge was to eradicate the debt he brought into the marriage, encountered what they thought was serious trouble when their 1962 Porsche got hit by a pickup truck. Max drove the car to work every day, and not only was it his only means of transportation but he loved it and would do anything to save it. They were frantic. "It's going to cost $900 to have it fixed," Max moaned. "We don't have $900," wailed Liz, "but we have to have it fixed."

The answer was simple: they had to find a cheaper repair shop. The couple made a game of finding the cheapest estimate and then got referrals. They got the work done for $600. They didn't really have $600 either, but the car did need to be fixed. Instead of shelling out $900 for the first estimate from a pricy foreign auto body shop, they searched until they found a reliable shop at a lower price. With reserves they had begun to set aside for car repair and maintenance, and money that had been earmarked for debt reduction, they fixed the Porsche. The car repair slowed down their progress, but not to the point of obliteration.

Excuses, Excuses . . .

Setting up a family cash flow plan is relatively easy, but implementing it can be more difficult. It is simple to declare, in a zealous moment, that you will do something to curb spending; actually putting in practice your intentions is much harder. You know the decision is sound, but now you have to act.

"We've decided to sell the computer to save $100 a month," said David Miller. Two weeks later, the Millers still had the computer and were facing another installment payment.

They didn't have a buyer because they hadn't advertised the computer. They had to give themselves a deadline to post an ad in the newspapers.

"We're going to spend $50 less a month on eating out," said Andrea Moore. The idea is good, but it takes more than just *saying* you'll spend less money eating out. Deciding to eat at home means planning ahead. You may need to spend an extra ten minutes in the morning discussing what you'll have for dinner, who's going to pick up the groceries, who's going to cook, and who's going to clean up. Maybe it's a simple matter of remembering to take meat out of the freezer before you leave for work. Andrea laughed once at their attempts to eat in. "We went grocery shopping together on Saturday, shopped shrewdly, and stocked the freezer for the week," she said. "Then we kept forgetting to take the chicken out to thaw. So, we ended up going out. For a while there we were actually spending more money on food because we were buying twice—once for eating at home, once for eating out."

"We'll put the kids in public school." The Millers again. Although the reputation of the local schools was one reason they moved to their neighborhood, they really knew little about the quality of the schools. To decide whether to make the switch from private to public, they had to assess the district and talk to other parents. The Millers finally assigned themselves specific tasks because they found they were talking a lot and not taking action.

"We'll curb impulse spending," said Henry and Jennifer Owens. That meant Henry had to stop buying so many books. It also meant that Jennifer had to stop buying a new pair of jeans every few weeks. They made a pact not to purchase anything on the first sighting. If a consumer good tempted them, they would come home and discuss it. They found that on second consideration, they often didn't really *want* what had attracted them.

If somehow your plan runs awry, you may be able to fix it with little trouble. Sometimes your problem may be simple arithmetic; or it could be that you were overly ambitious and need to reassess your goals and schedule.

But for some basic problems consider these solutions:

"We seem to have lost track of some money somewhere."

Ask yourself: Did you deposit all of your paychecks? Did you take back "less cash" that you forgot to record?

Suggested solution: Agree to deposit paychecks within a day of receiving them. Update your checkbook immediately, and take cash out only as you've agreed.

"We're getting late notices on bills and are being charged inordinate interest fees."

Ask yourself: Do you pay your bills on time?

Suggested solution: Note due date of bills, set specific times twice a month to pay bills, and pay them on time.

"We did everything you said to do, and we're still $300 short of our needs. Why?"

Ask yourself: Are your goals unrealistic, or have you made mathematical errors? Have some expenses increased that are unrecorded?

Suggested solution: Reevaluate your goals, and make sure what you wrote in the plan was the true picture. Look for ways to reduce expenses. Check your automatic debits, including ATM transactions. Make sure you log all changes as soon as you are notified. For example, if your adjustable mortgage payment is automatically debited from your checking account, and the payment rises or falls, modify your plan immediately to reflect the change.

Into the Future

Long-term success ultimately rests on communication and consistency. If you and your spouse share common goals and are actively directing and designing your family financial situation, you are already successful—no matter if your goal is two months or two years away. New habits and attitudes will sustain you through the difficulties.

Above all, give it time. There is no set schedule for concrete results or rewards. The first benefit is the satisfaction of having taken a positive, proactive step, of shifting from default to design. You'll feel good, and that's a big reward. The monetary satisfaction comes later when you see your savings account grow or your debt evaporate. We hope that this plan can act in many ways for you, from clearing up the papers on your desk and forging healthy habits to effecting a return to personal power and peace of mind.

CHECKPOINT 9

Success is a process, not an end or a means to an end. In reading this book, you have already begun the process. Your attitudes have begun to change; your perspectives have shifted. Now, to move forward, you must implement the plan. Develop good habits that reinforce your goals and new direction. Regularly scheduled monthly and biweekly meetings and visual tools will help.

Don't be afraid of setbacks, pitfalls, or emergencies. They come with the territory; they're part of the process. There is no such thing as failure. Temporary setbacks are not reason to throw away the plan in permanent frustration.

1. Assess your inventory of tools.
2. Review your filing system and consider reorganizing it as outlined earlier in this chapter.
3. Design progress charts to help stimulate enthusiasm: pictures, graphs, collages.
4. Make plans for and schedule your monthly meetings.
5. Create a family cash flow plan binder.

Identify the emotional or economic pitfalls that could occur for you in long-term management of your plan. Make provisions now for how you would deal with these situations.

EPILOGUE

Keeping the Spirit Alive

We'll say it again:

> There is almost nothing so exciting as falling madly in
> love, indulging in fantasies of the perfect life together,
> making the commitment, getting married, and beginning
> to build your dreams. The togetherness is exhilarating.
> And while you may not be the least bit interested in
> talking about finances, you notice one dramatic change:
> your income has increased, perhaps even doubled as a
> two-career couple. It's like a bonus for getting married.

Having two incomes *is* a bonus. If you live by design instead of
by default, with your eyes focused on your common goals, you
can experience the thrill that two incomes can bring. The whole
is greater than the sum of the parts. And if there is power to
having two incomes, there is more power in joining together as
a team. Now you can fulfill the dreams you thought should come
true when you originally combined your incomes. Instead of being a big headache, having two incomes becomes a way to meet
goals and challenges and have fun together and be fulfilled.

As partners, you have begun to pursue your common goals and make your dreams reality. You have begun to see just how rich you are, and you have begun to measure success as a process and a feeling of satisfaction, not a monetary measurement. You have taken the first steps toward liberating yourselves from debt and toward achieving the goals you really want. There will be payoffs and fulfillment every step of the way as you implement your plan, establishing and funding the necessary savings accounts and making your spending choices to reflect your new, healthier habits. Every small achievement is a big win.

Your diligence will lead you to the day of celebration—the day you actually achieve your primary and highest goal. Imagine the thrill of signing your escrow papers, of walking into the house you just bought, with your first armload of boxes. Imagine the feeling of awe you'll have when your baby is born after you've carefully planned and awaited his or her birth. Imagine the excitement of getting off the airplane in the country you've planned to visit. Imagine the sense of relief when you pay off the final balance of your credit card and can be assured you will pay any new balance off, in full each month, from here on out.

These are realistic aspirations. You can achieve these things if they are your primary goals, your burning desires. And it doesn't stop there. When you accomplish one goal, you can start on another. It's an exciting adventure to live your life with challenge and achievement together.

You have embarked on a commitment that becomes central to your lives. It's not just an issue of money. What is important is the happiness you have, the common goals, the delight you share in pursuing those goals. As you share, now you must stay with the plan. Don't get discouraged. The seed has been planted, keep it watered and watch it grow. Seek new and exciting ways to keep it vibrant and alive, and the harvest will be bountiful.

Don't worry about being perfect—accept your mistakes. The goal and the vision are more important than anything else. You are ready for this challenge and for the excitement and fulfillment that comes with it. You are motivated; you understand your goals. You can do it!

Everyone has value—that's the underlying message of this book. We invite you to acknowledge how valuable a service you provide to others. Taking inventory of your talents and abilities and your compassions will provide consistent self-motivation. When you have greater respect for yourself, your marriage or partnership, and your goals, you will direct your energy toward managing all areas of your life with reverence and efficiency.

Today, more than ever, we cannot afford to ignore our financial responsibilities. Being accountable for our successes takes the place of feeling like a financial victim. We need to learn to succeed so that we can be confident enough to manage our own families and help make this a better place for our children. You and your family count!

By communicating and working together on your goals and management of money, you are making a commitment to each other to succeed. This pattern influences other areas of your marriage in a positive way. As surveys show, money is the number-one issue in marriage today. Your willingness to have your cash management be healthy and productive will enable you to support any project or dream that you desire.

Richer than you dreamed . . . not just a state of mind, but a reality.

APPENDIX

The Family Cash Flow Plan

Welcome to the family cash flow plan—the foundation of the material we've covered in this book. The plan has been designed to help you manage your cash flow, attend to the payment of bills on time, save and accumulate necessary funds, and hold other pertinent financial data. To maintain your data in one easily accessible place, we suggest you use a three-ring binder with dividers for the three primary sections: income, expense, and backup data.

Primary Motivations and Payoffs

The development of the plan is based on your primary motivations and payoffs, those values and goals that will help you achieve satisfaction with your money. Specifically, your motivations and payoffs are addressed in two areas: the feelings or emotions that you have regarding various issues, and the material objects or conditions that are the manifestation of these issues, such as getting out of debt or buying a home.

Motivations occur in two ways: either you are motivated to

correct or eliminate a feeling or situation (directed from), or you are motivated to achieve a certain feeling or goal (directed toward). The information on this form is used to design the plan to focus your spending on the areas of greatest value or motivation.

Income

The income section of the plan consists of three pages. The first page is Projected Income, on which you identify your combined projected income, both on an annual and a monthly basis, with gross and net figures. In many categories, your gross and net will be the same because no taxes are withheld. All applicable sources of income are to be entered. After recording the individual sources, total each column. These figures give you a comprehensive overview of your income.

The next page is Actual Monthly Income, a ready-to-use form that shows a list of possible sources from which you receive income during the course of a month or a year. The information is entered in the proper category under the proper month once the money is actually received.

The third page is Actual Deductions from Income, a fairly comprehensive list of deductions typically taken out of a paycheck. It is important to know where all of your dollars are spent—not just the net pay.

Expenses

The Expense Guide provided in the plan helps to itemize monthly fixed and variable operating expenses, household expenses, debt payments (as listed on the Debts and Liabilities form), periodic/nonmonthly expenses, and savings needs. We recommend you create your own expense guide by purchasing fourteen-column ledger paper from your local office supplies store. Refer to the Expense Guide sample in this appendix for recommended layout of headings and expense descriptions. Please note that the first column is where your projected figures will be entered. The remaining columns will reflect actual dollars spent in each specific month. We suggest using your checkbook register and recent bills to determine amounts for your "projected" column. Begin with your normal fixed and variable operating expenses, then enter estimates of your average monthly household expenses. In some cases, such as household expenses or periodic/nonmonthly expenses, you may need to estimate figures for which you do not have exact amounts. These estimates can always be adjusted if they turn out to be inaccurate.

In order to obtain all, and accurate, monthly debt payments for entry on the Expense Guide, complete the Debts and Liabilities form, which includes credit cards, loans, taxes due, and miscellaneous items such as health club loans, doctor bills, and other outstanding obligations you are paying off. The information entered on this form is the total debt balance outstanding, the interest rate, the monthly payment, and the date the payment is due. When you complete this list, enter the correct monthly payment figures on the corresponding lines of the debt portion of your Expense Guide.

To this point, you have entered all normal monthly expenses. From here, you will address expenses that do not occur on a regular monthly basis, and, therefore, require monthly savings. As indicated on the Expense Guide, there are four distinct categories or purposes for savings: One to Four Payments a Year, Periodic/Nonmonthly Payments, Reserve, and Investment and Major Purchases.

The first category—One to Four Payments a Year—is for known expenses that come up during the year, either quarterly, semiannually, or annually. In most cases, you can identify the amount and perhaps even the date when these items are due, thereby coming to a total that you need for the entire year. Divide each annual figure by twelve to determine the amount to put aside each month. Enter each monthly amount on the appropriate line of the Expense Guide. When the payment comes due, simply make transfers to your checking account from your savings account and make the payment.

The second category—Periodic/Nonmonthly—is administered the same way as the first. You determine what you need on an annual basis, then divide by twelve, enter it on your Expense Guide, and save that amount each month. As these categories are for expenses that occur sporadically throughout the year, the amounts to save will range from the minimum needed to a preferred amount.

The target amount for the third category—Reserve—is determined differently. First, you must decide how much you need in actual liquidity to make up for loss of income due to disability, unemployment, or other reasons that prevent you from earning income. Some people want to save only a month's worth of income; others may consider several months.

Next, determine how much money you need to cover all of the various deductibles applicable for insurance claims—medical, dental, life, disability, auto, home, property, or tenant.

Finally, determine how much you need for repair and replacement of things you own. This figure ought to reflect the age and reliability of the equipment or appliances in your home. If your roof leaked last winter, it might be wise to build in a provision for repair or replacement.

Together, these three figures—income, deductibles, repair and replacement—represent the total amount you will need for the Reserve fund. Unlike the first two categories, this account can be built up over one to three years. Determine what period of time is realistic for your situation, and enter an amount to save each month on the Reserve line. In a year or two, you should review and reassess your target amount. Once you have reached the target amount, you will no longer need to add to your Reserve fund. Only in the event of an emergency will you need to use these funds. Then, just as with the other categories, you will transfer the needed amount into your checking account, make the payment, and then replenish the account over a reasonable period of time.

The fourth category of savings—Investment and Major

Backup Data

There are two forms that comprise backup data. The first form is a Financial Statement. In the left column are all of the assets you own—including cash and savings accounts, real estate, securities, retirement funds, and personal property. The liability side lists your obligations and amounts you owe for credit cards, personal loans, family loans, bank loans, and balances on mortgages and taxes.

The column totals will indicate total assets and total liabilities. To determine your net worth, subtract liabilities from assets.

The second form—Insurance Summary—includes all information regarding types of insurance, carrier, cost per year, and coverage highlights that address the various insurance programs you have. These data are usually obtained by reviewing your policy or calling your insurance agent. The information is entered here for reference as you design and assemble your cash flow plan.

The technical part of the plan may be somewhat tedious, particularly if you have little experience with keeping a ledger. But try to remember, as you are compiling all of your financial information, that you are working together to achieve your dreams. As a couple, you and your goals deserve the attention you direct to the data. Be supportive of each other as you compile the information, and set your target amounts for saving. If the exercise becomes frustrating, set it aside for a few hours, or even a day, but keep in mind the need to build this foundation of hard financial data so that you can plan your future and realize your dreams.

When you complete the family cash flow plan, you will have a strategy for taking control of your family spending and achieving your common and individual goals. You will be well on your way to becoming richer than you dreamed!

due, simply make transfers to your checking account from your savings account and make the payment.

The second category—Periodic/Nonmonthly—is administered the same way as the first. You determine what you need on an annual basis, then divide by twelve, enter it on your Expense Guide, and save that amount each month. As these categories are for expenses that occur sporadically throughout the year, the amounts to save will range from the minimum needed to a preferred amount.

The target amount for the third category—Reserve—is determined differently. First, you must decide how much you need in actual liquidity to make up for loss of income due to disability, unemployment, or other reasons that prevent you from earning income. Some people want to save only a month's worth of income; others may consider several months.

Next, determine how much money you need to cover all of the various deductibles applicable for insurance claims—medical, dental, life, disability, auto, home, property, or tenant.

Finally, determine how much you need for repair and replacement of things you own. This figure ought to reflect the age and reliability of the equipment or appliances in your home. If your roof leaked last winter, it might be wise to build in a provision for repair or replacement.

Together, these three figures—income, deductibles, repair and replacement—represent the total amount you will need for the Reserve fund. Unlike the first two categories, this account can be built up over one to three years. Determine what period of time is realistic for your situation, and enter an amount to save each month on the Reserve line. In a year or two, you should review and reassess your target amount. Once you have reached the target amount, you will no longer need to add to your Reserve fund. Only in the event of an emergency will you need to use these funds. Then, just as with the other categories, you will transfer the needed amount into your checking account, make the payment, and then replenish the account over a reasonable period of time.

The fourth category of savings—Investment and Major

Purchases—represents such needs as retirement, children's education, major vacations, second home, cars, or furniture—costlier items that will require time for which to save. Once you've determined this figure, you have a target for upcoming expenses and will build this account based on available funds.

(To fund these categories of savings, you will need to open two to four accounts in which to deposit funds. If you'd like to keep the number of accounts to a minimum, you may want to open one account for the One to Four Payments a Year category and the Periodic/Nonmonthly category and one account for the Reserve fund and the Investments and Major Purchases fund. You still will keep separate records for each category, but the money itself can be deposited into the two accounts. We combined the first two categories because they are meant for spending; there will be frequent transfers to your checking account. The second two funds are designed to be left alone for long periods of time. Using two savings accounts works if you have the ability to keep good records and maintain self-discipline. However, if you tend to "borrow" too readily from your savings accounts, you may need to open four separate accounts to reduce the temptation to borrow from yourself.)

You have now entered all expenses that occur in your family throughout the year, monthly and periodic. Each category has a subtotal line. Calculate all of your subtotals and enter them on the corresponding lines. Then calculate the grand total by adding all your subtotals and enter this figure on the grand total line. This grand total figure represents a monthly average of your annual expenditures.

At the end of each month, use your checkbook register to tally the amounts spent in each category. Enter those amounts on the appropriate lines. For payments to credit cards, we recommend you tally charges made by category—clothes, gifts, restaurants, or gasoline—and enter the amount per category on the appropriate line on the Expense Guide. Below the grand total line, enter deposits made to savings that month in each of the four savings categories.

FEELINGS/EMOTIONS

Directed Toward

Directed From

_____

_____

_____

_____

_____

_____

_____

_____

_____

_____

_____

_____

LIFESTYLE/GOALS/RESULTS

Directed Toward

Directed From

_____

_____

_____

_____

_____

_____

_____

_____

_____

_____

_____

_____

Date _____ Initials _____

PRIMARY MOTIVATIONS AND PAYOFFS

FEELINGS/EMOTIONS

Directed Toward   **Directed From**

_____   _____

_____   _____

_____   _____

_____   _____

_____   _____

_____   _____

LIFESTYLE/GOALS/RESULTS

Directed Toward   **Directed From**

_____   _____

_____   _____

_____   _____

_____   _____

_____   _____

_____   _____

Date _____ Initials _____

Income	Monthly		Annual	
	Net	*Gross*	*Net*	*Gross*
His Salary				
Her Salary				
His Free-lance Earnings				
Her Free-lance Earnings				
Commissions				
Bonuses				
Child Support				
Interest				
Dividends				
Loan Proceeds				
Rental Property				
Other _____				
_____				
Total				

Date _____ Initials _____

||| ACTUAL MONTHLY INCOME |||

Year:	Jan	Feb	Mar	Apr	May
His Salary (net)					
Her Salary (net)					
His Free-lance Earnings					
Her Free-lance Earnings					
Commissions					
Bonuses					
Child Support					
Interest					
Dividends					
Loan Proceeds					
Rental Property					
Tax Refund					
Other Sources of Income					
Total Monthly Income					

Jun	Jul	Aug	Sep	Oct	Nov	Dec	Total

ACTUAL DEDUCTIONS FROM INCOME

Year of Deduction:	Jan	Feb	Mar	Apr	May
Federal Income Tax (FIT)					
State Income Tax (SIT)					
Social Security (FICA)					
State Disability (SDI)					
Life/Disability Insurance					
Health Insurance					
Pension Plan					
Profit Sharing					
Savings					
Stock Option Plan (ESOP)					
Contributions					
Loan Payment					
Union Dues					
Other					
Total					

Jun	Jul	Aug	Sep	Oct	Nov	Dec	Total

▐▐▐ EXPENSE GUIDE ▐▐▐

	PRO-JECTED EXPENSE	MO. 1 ACTUAL	MO. 2 ACTUAL	MO. 3 ACTUAL	YEAR-TO-DATE TOTALS

OPERATING EXPENSES—FIXED

	PRO-JECTED EXPENSE	MO. 1 ACTUAL	MO. 2 ACTUAL	MO. 3 ACTUAL	YEAR-TO-DATE TOTALS
AUTO LEASE					
CABLE TV					
CHILD CARE					
CHILDREN'S PROGRAMS					
INSURANCE					
AUTO					
DISABILITY					
HEALTH					
LIFE					
RENT					
SCHOOL TUITION					
SUBTOTALS—FIXED					

Date _____ Initials _____

	PRO-JECTED EXPENSE	MO. 1 ACTUAL	MO. 2 ACTUAL	MO. 3 ACTUAL	YEAR-TO-DATE TOTALS

OPERATING EXPENSES—VARIABLE

CHILDREN'S MISC. NEEDS					
CLUB DUES/EXTRAS					
GARBAGE					
GAS/ELECTRIC					
HOUSEKEEPER/GARDENER					
POOL/SPA SERVICE					
TELEPHONE					
WATER					
SUBTOTALS—VARIABLE					

EXPENSE GUIDE

	PRO-JECTED EXPENSE	MO. 1 ACTUAL	MO. 2 ACTUAL	MO. 3 ACTUAL	YEAR-TO-DATE TOTALS

HOUSEHOLD EXPENSES

	PRO-JECTED EXPENSE	MO. 1 ACTUAL	MO. 2 ACTUAL	MO. 3 ACTUAL	YEAR-TO-DATE TOTALS
FOOD/MISC. HOUSEHOLD ITEMS					
FOOD OUT/RESTAURANTS					
ENTERTAINMENT					
LAUNDRY/DRY CLEANING					
GAS/PARKING/TOLLS/TICKETS					
PUBLIC TRANSPORTATION					
BABYSITTING					
PET CARE					
SELF-CARE (e.g., Manicure, Facial)					
COUNSELING/THERAPY					
MINOR MEDICAL					
MISC. OTHER (e.g., Postage, Books, CDs)					
SUBTOTALS—HOUSEHOLD					

DEBT PAYMENTS	PRO-JECTED EXPENSE	MO. 1 ACTUAL	MO. 2 ACTUAL	MO. 3 ACTUAL	YEAR-TO-DATE TOTALS
MORTGAGE #1					
MORTGAGE #2					
EQUITY LINE					
INSTALLMENT LOANS					
AUTO #1					
AUTO #2					
COMPUTER/FURNITURE					
BANK/CREDIT UNION					
PRIVATE/FAMILY #1					
PRIVATE/FAMILY #2					
STUDENT LOANS					
CREDIT CARD PAYMENTS					
DEPT. STORE #1					
DEPT. STORE #2					
DEPT. STORE #3					
VISA/MASTERCARD #1					
VISA/MASTERCARD #2					
VISA/MASTERCARD #3					
GAS CARD #1					
GAS CARD #2					
TAXES					
FEDERAL					
STATE					
DOCTORS/DENTISTS					
SUBTOTALS—DEBT					

EXPENSE GUIDE

	PRO-JECTED EXPENSE	MO. 1 ACTUAL	MO. 2 ACTUAL	MO. 3 ACTUAL	YEAR-TO-DATE TOTALS

ONE TO FOUR PAYMENTS A YEAR EXPENSES

	PRO-JECTED EXPENSE	MO. 1 ACTUAL	MO. 2 ACTUAL	MO. 3 ACTUAL	YEAR-TO-DATE TOTALS
AUTO REGISTRATION					
DUES/LICENSES/PUBLICATIONS					
INSURANCE					
AUTO					
HEALTH/DENTAL					
DISABILITY					
LIFE					
HOME					
PROPERTY/RENTAL					
TAXES					
FEDERAL					
STATE					
PROPERTY					
TAX PREPARATION/PROFESSIONAL FEES					
SUBTOTALS/AMOUNT SAVED PER MONTH					

PERIODIC/NONMONTHLY EXPENSES

CLOTHING					
GIFTS					
TRAVEL/VACATION					
FURNITURE/APPLIANCES					
CONTRIBUTIONS					
CONTINUING EDUCATION					
HOME MAINTENANCE/REPAIR					
AUTO MAINTENANCE/REPAIR					
HEALTH MAINTENANCE					
SUBTOTALS/AMOUNT SAVED PER MONTH					

	PRO-JECTED EXPENSE	MO. 1 ACTUAL	MO. 2 ACTUAL	MO. 3 ACTUAL	YEAR-TO-DATE TOTALS

SAVINGS

RESERVE					
INVESTMENT AND MAJOR PURCHASES					

GRAND TOTAL EXPENSES	$	$	$	$	$

DEPOSITS TO SAVINGS

ONE TO FOUR PAYMENTS A YEAR EXPENSES					
PERIODIC/NONMONTHLY EXPENSES					
RESERVE					
INVESTMENT AND MAJOR PURCHASES					

DEBTS AND LIABILITIES

	TOTAL BALANCE	INTEREST RATE	MONTHLY PAYMENT	DATE DUE

I. CREDIT CARDS

	TOTAL BALANCE	INTEREST RATE	MONTHLY PAYMENT	DATE DUE
1.				
2.				
3.				
4.				
5.				
6.				
7.				
8.				
SUBTOTAL				

II. LOANS

	TOTAL BALANCE	INTEREST RATE	MONTHLY PAYMENT	DATE DUE
1.				
2.				
3.				
4.				
5.				
SUBTOTAL				

	TOTAL BALANCE	INTEREST RATE	MONTHLY PAYMENT	DATE DUE

III. TAXES

	TOTAL BALANCE	INTEREST RATE	MONTHLY PAYMENT	DATE DUE
1. Federal—year_____				
2. State—year _____				
3. Property—year _____				
4. Other _____				
SUBTOTAL				

IV. MISCELLANEOUS

1.				
2.				
3.				
4.				
5.				
6.				
SUBTOTAL				

GRAND TOTAL				

FINANCIAL STATEMENT

Assets—What I Own

Cash in Savings Accounts	$_____
Cash in Money Market Accounts	$_____
Cash Value–Life Insurance Policies	$_____
Certificate of Deposits	$_____
Mutual Funds	$_____
Current Market Value of Stocks, Bonds and Other Securities	$_____
Market Value of Residence	$_____
Market Value of Income Property	$_____
Market Value of Recreation Property	$_____
Equity in Limited Partnerships	$_____
Equity in Trust Accounts	$_____
Current Value of IRAs	$_____
Current Value of Keogh Accounts	$_____
Current Value of Pension Plans	$_____
Current Value of Profit Sharings	$_____
Market Value of Automobiles	$_____
Estimated Value of Personal Property (such as equipment, collectibles, furnishings, jewelry, etc.)	$_____
Other Assets_____	$_____
_____	$_____
Total Assets	$_____

Liabilities—What I Owe

Credit Cards	$_____
Personal Loans	$_____
Family Loans	$_____
Bank Loans	$_____
Mortgages	$_____
Past-Due Taxes: Property Tax	$_____
Federal Income Tax	$_____
State Income Tax	$_____
Other_____	$_____

To determine your net worth, subtract what you owe from what you own.

Total Liabilities	$_____

Total Net Worth $_____

INSURANCE SUMMARY

Type of Insurance	Carrier	Cost/Year	Coverage Highlights	
Health	_____	$_____	Deductible	$_____
			Maximum out of Pocket	$_____
			Maximum Benefit	$_____
			Type of Policy _____	
Dental	_____	$_____	Deductible	$_____
			Maximum Benefit	$_____
Disability	_____	$_____	Benefit Amount	$_____/mo.
			Benefit Period	$_____/yrs.
			Benefit Starts After	_____days
State Disability	_____	$_____	Benefit Amount	$_____/mo.
			Benefit Period	$_____/yrs.
			Benefit Starts After	_____days
Life	_____	$_____	Total Face Value of Policy $_____	
			☐ Term ☐ Whole/Universal	
			Beneficiary_____	
Auto	_____	$_____	Collision— Deductible	$_____
			Comprehensive— Deductible	$_____
			Amount of Liability	$_____
Property and Liability	_____	$_____	Deductible	$_____
			Amount of Liability	$_____
			Replacement Value	$_____

INDEX

167